SCIENCE
FOR PRIMARY SCHOOLS
A core course

Teacher's Guide 1

(WLE) Ward Lock Educational

© S F King 1985

ISBN 0 7062 4364 1

First published 1985 by
Ward Lock Educational Co. Ltd.
47 Marylebone Lane
London W1M 6AX

Reprinted 1987

A member of the Ling Kee Group
Hong Kong · Taipei · Singapore · London · New York

Typeset by Dorchester Typesetting Group Ltd.
Printed by Netherwood Dalton & Co. Ltd. Huddersfield

Our thanks are due to Dorothy Diamond who acted as
series editor for *Science for Primary Schools.*

Contents

INTRODUCTION

Science for Primary Schools is a core course for junior school pupils aged between 7 and 11 years.

For each of the four years there are two Pupils' Books, a Teacher's Guide and a pack of Master-sheets which are used in conjunction with the Pupils' Books.

The Pupils' Books

In the first year books (1A and 1B) the ten themes are introduced. These are:

Book 1A	*Book 1B*
Time	Air
Water	Animals
Energy 1	Energy 2
Ourselves	Plants
Structures	Light and colour

These themes are developed during the succeeding years so that Pupils' Books 2A, 3A and 4A contain material based on the themes introduced in Book 1A, and Pupils' Books 2B, 3B and 4B contain material based on the themes introduced in Book 1B. Thus there is a vertical development of the ten themes throughout the four years.

In the first year books, which are aimed at seven-year-old pupils, the amount of text per page has been purposely kept to a minimum. Nevertheless, new words are introduced when necessary, so there is an increase in vocabulary during the year's work.

Similarly, in the books for years 2, 3 and 4, the text has been structured to suit the average pupil aged 8, 9 and 10 years. The amount of text per page increases from year to year as does the complexity of the sentences used, although in all the books simplicity has been a keynote of the Activities.

Illustrations are frequently used in conjunction with the text. In Books 1A and 1B these are simple and mainly pictorial, but over the four years there is a gradual evolution of the illustrations towards the vertical cross section diagram much used in science. The cross sectional diagram is used because it is simple to draw and also because it shows the relationships between the various parts of the apparatus clearly. It is hoped that, by the time the pupils reach the end of the course, they will be able to draw and understand 'scientific diagrams'.

In the next part of the *Teacher's Guide* there is a consideration of what is meant by the term 'science' when we are teaching 7-11 year old children. The development of science, from simple observation and fair testing with the younger children, to the designing of experiments with the older children, is taken stage by stage in order to keep in line with the mental development of the children during these four years.

As is stated later in this book, science is a practical subject which must be learnt at first hand as far as possible. Books are an essential adjunct to this practical learning, but it is by carrying out the Activities that the children will really learn. And they will not just learn science. The Activities provide the practice essential for the development of many skills and concepts. By reading the text the pupils will be practising their reading skills and increasing their vocabulary and general understanding of the English language. When recording the Activities the children will be involved in ordering their ideas and practising their writing skills. Sometimes graphs have to be drawn and number relationships calculated: these develop mathematical skills. In a similar way, the ability to handle simple pieces of equipment, to work within a small group, and to work co-operatively with other children, are all skills which must be practised if they are to develop. Other skills such as the measurement of length, surface area, time, volume and weight all need practice which is provided by the Activities in the Pupils' Books. For a more detailed discussion of the science skills which can be fostered in children, a paper produced by the School Natural Science Society entitled *Primary School Science Skills* should be consulted. It is available from the Association for Science Education whose address is given at the back of this book.

The Teacher's Guides

A Teacher's Guide is provided for each of the four years. In these books the themes are discussed in order and within each theme the Activities are described in detail. The equipment needed to carry out each Activity is described, and in some cases construction notes are given for those teachers who wish to make their own apparatus. In all cases each piece of equipment is easily available from various suppliers. Much use is made of household items which are generally thrown away: plastic lemonade bottles, washing-up liquid bottles and yoghurt pots are examples.

The equipment needed to carry out the Activities has been purposely kept simple. Much of it is already available in schools. Where it is necessary to purchase equipment, addresses of suppliers are given at the back of each Teacher's Guide.

The Mastersheets

The Mastersheets are copyright-free provided that they are used to make copies for use within the school which purchased them. They can either be photocopied or a stencil prepared from them which can be used to duplicate the number of copies required.

The General Mastersheets common to all four years include individual and class record sheets, a simple one metre tape measure, centimetre-squared paper and a twenty centimetre ruler marked in half centimetres.

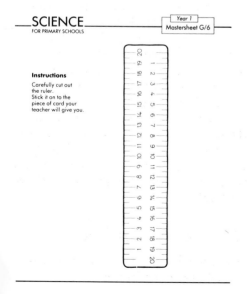

Children often have difficulty in drawing out tables for recording the measurements and observations obtained from the Activities, so these tables are available on Mastersheets.

The General Mastersheets also contain a word list. This list contains words which may be new to the children and words which they frequently mis-spell. The word list can be fixed into the children's notebooks or folders so that it can be referred to when they are writing up their records.

At the beginning of this introduction it was stated that *Science for Primary Schools* is a core course. The term 'core course' is used because the course is not intended to include *all* the work in science which might be covered in a junior school. It does, however, provide a core from which other work can easily be developed. Some ideas on how the work in *Science for Primary Schools* can be followed up are given in this and the other Teacher's Guides. No doubt other ideas for follow-up work will occur to many teachers using the course.

The aim of *Science for Primary Schools* is to provide interesting and varied Activities which will give a framework upon which the scientific work of pupils in junior schools can be built.

SCIENCE IN THE JUNIOR SCHOOL

Since science was first introduced into the curriculum of some junior schools about thirty years ago, there has been much discussion about what the teaching of science to this age group really means. This discussion will probably continue for many years to come, but in this section a concensus of the views held at the present time will be given. This concensus also represents to a certain extent a personal view.

The main aim of science in the junior school is to introduce pupils to the 'scientific method' of working. It is not the aim of junior science to implant in the children's minds a mass of so-called 'scientific facts'. By scientific facts or knowledge is meant that knowledge which has been accumulated through the application of scientific method. The value of this scientific information to the junior school pupil is very limited, although, by the time the child has reached the end of the junior school, he or she will have incidentally accumulated a quite considerable body of knowledge from the work done in science.

What is meant, then, by the 'scientific method'? It can be divided into a number of steps or stages, of which the first is the making of a series of observations which may take the form of measurements. These observations are made carefully and accurately. Many of the Activities in Books 1A, 1B, 2A and 2B are structured to teach children how observations should be made and how they should be recorded. It is to be hoped that, in addition to the structured observation-making activities in the Pupils' Books, other situations will arise in the classroom which can be investigated. The next stage is the posing of questions arising from the observations and then trying to find the answers by means of tests of various sorts. Another way in which the investigation may proceed is by the formation of inferences from a review of the observations. The inference may take the form of a question or can be turned into a question. A simple example may clarify this point. Suppose some children have been looking for woodlice in the playground or park. They find some woodlice and note that they are all found under rocks and stones. This observation is noted. An inference can be drawn from this observation: that all woodlice prefer living in dark places. This inference can be questioned on two counts:

Can we test *all* woodlice?
How can we find out if they prefer to live in dark places?

The answer to the first question is a definite no. It would be impossible to test all woodlice. On the other hand, if we test as large a number as possible, we should be able to come to a conclusion such as 'We found that, of the two hundred woodlice we tested, one hundred and ninety-five preferred dark places'. A further point which may be discovered from associated reading and looking at pictures of woodlice in books, is that there is more than one species of woodlouse. It is, therefore, necessary to test out woodlice which belong to the same species. Further testing could establish whether woodlice in general, not just the first species discovered, prefer to live in light or dark places. Other observations made on the environment of the woodlice may include the fact that they all seem

---

ENERGY 1

Activity 23   HOW HIGH AND HOW FAR?

You will need

the things from
Activity 22
Mastersheet 15

5 cm

- Make the slope 5 cm high at the top.
  Put the car at the top of the slope.
  Let it go.
  How far does it go?
  Do this twice more.

  Write the distances in the table on Mastersheet 15.

- Do the same with the slope 10 cm high, then 15 cm high, then 20 cm high.
  Did the car go further as you made the slope steeper?

  What did you have to do to make the car move?

- Put the car on a flat board.
  Let it go.
  Does it move?

  Write down what you did and what you found out.
  A drawing would help.

page 31

6

to live in damp and cold or cool places. This again can lead to further investigation.

The testing process is in itself very important. For example, if, as in the previous paragraph, the preferences of woodlice are being tested, we must ensure that we take one aspect of their environment at a time. Then, keeping all other factors constant, we can test the preference for this aspect alone. For example, suppose we are going to investigate the preference of the woodlice as regards light or dark. When we test the preference for a light or a dark situation we must ensure that the dampness and the temperature are kept constant throughout the testing. Similarly, when testing their preference for damp or dry situations, we must make sure that the situations are equally illuminated and are at the same temperature.

In this investigation, the illumination, the humidity and the temperature are called the variables. It is an important part of the scientific method of investigation that we isolate the variables and investigate the effect of one variable at a time. From the investigations into woodlouse preferences we can, by isolating the variables, come to a conclusion as to the type of environment a woodlouse prefers.

The isolation of variables is difficult for the younger children and they will need plenty of help from the teacher in this work. Even with older junior school children, considerable guidance will be needed if they are to isolate the variables and investigate one at a time. In Book 4A the children are encouraged to look at a simple pendulum and to see that there are three variables which could be investigated:

1 the length of the pendulum
2 the mass of the bob
3 the amplitude (or angle) of swing.

From here the children can investigate these variables and finally come to a conclusion about the way a pendulum swings.

Here is a further example of an inference which might be drawn from an observation and then tested to find if it is correct or not. We see two people at the side of the road looking under the bonnet of a car. What inference can be drawn from this simple observation? That the car

has broken down and the two people are trying to repair it? Or that the car is brand new and they are looking at the new engine? How can we tell which inference is correct? The best way is to go up to the people and ask! Another way would be to eavesdrop on the conversation and from this we should soon realise which of the two previous inferences was correct.

Sometimes an investigation may be initiated by direct means. This is often the case with the Activities in the Pupils' Books. The children are asked a question such as 'Which ball is the best bouncer?'. This leads to a discussion of what we mean by 'best'? Does it mean the ball which bounces highest, or the ball which bounces the greatest number of times? Both of these could be investigated. Incidentally, a discussion about the original question can usefully lead on to a consideration of whether some questions are good questions or not. What is meant by the 'best' washing powder? Or what is meant by 'good weather'? The answer to the latter question will depend very much on who is asking the question and in what situation the question is being asked. For a farmer in the middle of haymaking the answer will be dry and warm weather, while a gardener whose garden is badly in need of rain may well say that 'good weather' is a downpour of rain.

Care in the formulation of questions is important. Some questions can be answered by investigations using the scientific method. Other questions do not lend themselves to the application of the scientific method. A typical question of this sort is 'Do you like this picture?'. This sort of question can only be answered subjectively.

To summarise what has been said, we can show the way the scientific method is used in the form of a simple diagram:

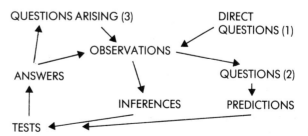

The system can be entered at a number of different places. The starting point from using the Pupils' Books will be at (1) or (2), while the starting point from questions asked in the classroom will be (3).

Scientific observations have one important characteristic which distinguishes them from other observations: the same observation can be repeated any number of times. If a pupil measures the length of his or her desk and finds it to be 56cm, then this constitutes a simple scientific observation. It is an objective observation. If, on the other hand, a child (or anybody else for that matter), states that his or her favourite colour is blue, then this is an unscientific and subjective observation. The person's preference may well alter with time and the reasons for the preference may be impossible to determine. If we collect together the colour preferences of a number of people at the same time, we can tell from these preferences which is the most popular and the least popular colour. These preferences, though, are only valid for that particular group of people at that particular time. This is rather similar to an opinion poll, which only shows people's preferences at a particular time. If the poll were carried out at a different time with the same people, it is very probable that the results would be different.

The making of observations is not as simple a process as some people think. Suppose we put a fly in front of a child who has no knowledge of insects and suggest that he or she writes down all that he or she can find out about the animal (i.e. records observations). It is unlikely that the child will write down all the characteristics of insects. The child may be fascinated with the colour or the size of the fly and ignore other facets of its structure. To observe properly and with insight requires previous knowledge or, at least, some external direction. For example, we might ask 'How many legs has the animal?', 'Has it got wings?' and so on. Or we might discuss the characteristics of an insect with the child beforehand and then ask the child whether the fly is an insect.

Another example of the importance of previous knowledge in observation is when a child is looking down a microscope. What the child sees will be directly related to what the child knows. If, for example, he or she is looking at a small piece of onion epidermis (skin), the child may well see a mass of interconnecting lines. On the other hand, if the child already knows that plants are made up of box-like structures called cells, the view down the microscope takes on an entirely different meaning. Similarly, if the child is looking at a human blood smear under the microscope, previous knowledge of the types of cell usually found in human blood makes the recognition of the smear much easier. With no previous knowledge the smear would be a complete mystery to the child. For a further, more detailed discussion about observation, the two chapters 'The Pump' and 'The Amiable Juice' in Jonathan Miller's book *The Body in Question* (published by Jonathan Cape, 1978) should be consulted.

Initial observation by children needs direction: children need starting points from which they can eventually make their own original observations.

CLASSROOM ORGANISATION

As science is a practical activity, the organisation of the work within the classroom and school is very important.

In the ideal situation the children would be working individually or occasionally with a partner. With the size of classes in many junior schools reaching the thirty-five to forty mark this is not often possible and therefore we have to divide the class into groups of three or four children. How these groups are made up can in itself pose a problem. Should all the children in one group be similar in their reading ability and their mathematical skills, or should the groups consist of children of mixed ability? One way of dividing the children into groups is to allow the children to decide how they will divide themselves up. This often results in groups which work well together, although there may be a problem to be resolved over the child with whom nobody in the class wants to work. Another way of producing the groups is for the teacher, with his or her comprehensive knowledge of the members of the class, to arrange the groups. The composition of the groups is important and perhaps the solution to the problem lies in a mixture of 'friends', abilities and professional judgement. Further, the groups need not be permanent: the composition of the groups could easily be varied as the occasion demands or when the teacher deems it to be necessary. One pitfall which should be avoided if possible is where, say, two children in a group of four take charge of the work, leaving the other two members of the group to act merely as passive spectators.

If the class size is, say, thirty-six, there could be either twelve groups of three or nine groups of four. Although the aim should be to have group size as small as possible, it is physically better to have nine groups rather than twelve. It is easier, for example, to collect together the equipment needed for nine groups than for twelve. Space in the classroom is another factor which must be considered. In most classrooms nine groups can be physically catered for, but twelve groups pose a much greater problem.

Once the number and composition of the groups has been settled, the next problem is how to distribute the equipment and to get the groups working. There are two main ways of tackling the Activities:

1 all the groups do the same Activity at the same time
2 the 'circus' arrangement.

Where all the groups are doing the same Activity at the same time, the number of sets of equipment required is obviously the same as the number of groups. This can prove to be expensive, though at times it is essential. It does mean that, as all groups are involved in the same Activity, discipline and order problems are rather easier to solve than when the 'circus' arrangement is used. It is essential that certain groups of Activities are followed through in a particular order, and, in this case, it is necessary for all groups to follow the same sequence of Activities at the same time. For example, the Activities described in the Water section of Book 1A depend on the order suggested being followed: the knowledge gained from one Activity is used in carrying out the next Activity. Similarly, the Activities in the Structures section of Book 1B must be carried out in the order given.

If all the groups do the same Activity at the same time, enough equipment for the groups must be collected together beforehand, allowing, if possible, one or two spare sets to cover possible breakages, etc. If time allows, the equipment can be placed in the working areas before the lesson starts. If this is not possible, then the equipment can be gathered together at one central distribution point.

The main disadvantage when the same Activity is being carried out by all the groups is the amount of apparatus required. A further disadvantage is that different groups finish the particular Activity at different times. This means that some groups will be working while others may be waiting impatiently to continue with the next piece of work. One solution to this problem is to provide follow-up work which can be done by the groups which finish early.

In the 'circus' arrangement, a number of Activities are set up at the same time. Each group carries out a different Activity. When one group has finished its particular Activity, it moves on to another one until, eventually, all groups have completed all the Activities. From the teacher's point of view, this means that all the apparatus for all the Activities has to be collected together before the circus can begin. However, only one set of equipment is needed for each Activity and, once the initial work of getting together the equipment has been done, there is usually a considerable length of time before a new set of equipment is needed.

The circus arrangement is best used when there are a number of Activities relating to the same theme, but the individual Activities do not depend on one another. As an example, the Activities in the Ourselves section of Book 1A all relate to the senses, but the Activity on smelling is independent of the Activity using the 'feelie box'.

It is best to have sufficient equipment available for each Activity to be set up twice. This allows for the different rates of working and ensures that all groups will be fully occupied all the time.

I prefer to use the circus method of working whenever possible. It makes for a lively, stimulating and interesting atmosphere in the classroom. It cannot always be used for the reasons stated above, but it is much more economical in the amount of equipment used. Its main disadvantage is that it requires a great deal of preparation beforehand. However, this is offset by the fact that, once the preparation for a circus has been done, there is usually a reasonable gap before the next circus begins or before a new set of Activities is started.

Before a circus is started it is necessary to discuss with the whole class each of the Activities in the circus. At the end of the circus, when all the groups have completed all the Activities, a further discussion should take place. During this follow-up discussion each Activity can be gone through. Finally, the total effect of the circus can be analysed.

On the few occasions when it is necessary to demonstrate an Activity, it is as well for the teacher to rehearse the Activity beforehand and to think carefully about the best way to present it to the class. A well organised and carried out demonstration can be a valuable lesson in itself. With most demonstrations it is possible to involve some members of the class. During the demonstration the teacher should show how the equipment can be arranged in an orderly manner and used properly and how the results are recorded correctly.

One reason for demonstrating an Activity is that it is considered too dangerous for the children to carry out. During the demonstration, the teacher can emphasise safety precautions and show how risks can be eliminated or kept to a minimum.

It may be necessary to demonstrate an Activity because there is insufficient apparatus for group work. In this case it is essential to involve as many members of the class as possible. As already stated, science is a practical subject learnt by 'doing' and not by passively watching somebody else.

Whether an Activity is demonstrated or carried out by the children may also be determined by the children themselves. Classes differ a great deal in their attitude and behaviour. Although we may feel quite confident that one class will carry out a particular Activity safely and properly, with another class we may feel that the risk is too great. It is up to the individual teacher to use his or her professional judgement in making this type of decision.

Many teachers express concern over the fact that an Activity may not 'work'. All Activities work, but some may not work in the manner we expect them to. The Activities in the Pupils' Books are all tried and tested and, provided reasonable care is taken, they will work, that is, show what we expect them to show. However, if an Activity does work, but not in the way we expected, then this provides an interesting investigation. What caused the Activity to work in this particular way rather than in the way we expected? The teacher may decide to investigate this with the class or group or to make a personal investigation.

It is strongly recommended that short notes are written up by the teacher after each Activity, particularly when the Activities are being worked through for the first time. These notes could include such items as the class/group response to the Activity, the source of the equipment and where it is stored, whether the Activity was easy to set up and whether it worked in the expected manner. Such notes can prove invaluable in a school, particularly to teachers new to this type of work.

One final statement. One of the reasons for my particular interest in science teaching is that the essential practical work with my classes has always been a source of interest and fun both for me and my classes. The pleasure derived from the work has always been a great stimulus to me to try to make my lessons more interesting and to try to incorporate new practical ideas whenever possible. These books are written to provide a base or starting point both for teachers and pupils. From this starting point I hope that a door may be opened into the fascinating world of science.

RECORDING

The recording of a scientific activity is an essential part of the scientific method. It is important to inform other people how an Activity was carried out, the equipment used to do this, the results or other observations made during the Activity and what was found out. It is also important that the pupils should learn to order their recording, and be able to describe in both words and pictures (diagrams) what was done and what the Activity demonstrated.

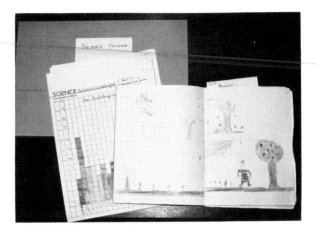

The first decision to be made by the teacher is whether the recording should be done in a book or on sheets of paper kept in a folder of some sort. There are advantages and disadvantages to both these methods.

The main advantage of using a book is that all the material is kept together in one place and is less likely to be mislaid. Furthermore, it is easier for the teacher to mark a book rather than a multitude of pieces of paper. The main disadvantage is the limits imposed by using a book. A book does not allow for much variation in the type of recording. In some cases the recording may best be done by a series of drawings which might be cramped and small within the confines of a normal school exercise book. Graphs may be drawn and these would have to be glued into the book. Pictures may be collected from newspapers and magazines to illustrate the work in progress and these, again, must be fixed into the book. These additions to the pages of the book will tend to split the cover and to make it untidy.

The main disadvantage of using a folder is that the loose sheets have a tendency to become dog-eared and dirty over a period of time. Some sheets will inevitably get lost and so the record will be incomplete. It is also quite difficult for the pupil to keep the loose sheets in order so that progression can be seen.

The best solution I have found to this problem is to use the advantages of both methods. In other words, each pupil has a notebook where the main writing and drawing is done, but also a folder in which are kept the larger sheets of paper and other subsidiary material.

Recording of scientific activities with children in the junior school can take many forms. With the youngest children who have only recently acquired reading and writing skills, too much writing should be avoided, though the value of practising these skills cannot be over-estimated. Simple pictures drawn by the children can not only provide a record for the pupils but can also tell us a great deal about what the child learnt from doing the Activity.

In the early stages of a course of this sort the pictures can be supplemented by a few simple sentences of explanation. Where lists or tables of results have been gathered, these should be added to the pictures and writing. Tables of results in Books 1A and 1B have been printed on the Mastersheets and these can either be fixed into notebooks or kept in a folder.

When numerical results have been gathered, they can be used to draw a simple histogram or bar graph, provided there is good reason for drawing the graph. The function of a graph is to show in a visual manner the relationships (or the lack of relationships) between the measurements made. In many cases a graph reveals relationships much more easily than merely looking at lists of figures. A good example of this type of graph is the one suggested in the Time section of Book 1A to illustrate the number of birthdays each month. It is important for the children to realise the importance of:

1 labelling both axes with the units used (e.g. months, number of birthdays)
2 giving the graph an explanatory title.

Any graph without these is incomplete and unscientific.

How a particular Activity is recorded will depend on the Activity itself, the class, the teacher and the particular school. It is for the teacher to make the final decision as to how exactly the Activity should be recorded, taking into account his or her knowledge of the children's capabilities and also the general attitude of the school towards this type of work. It is sometimes a good idea to ask the children to suggest the best way of making a record of a particular Activity.

Suggestions as to the sort of record which could be made for each Activity are given later in the book.

Then there is the problem of marking the children's work. Again this will depend on the prevailing attitudes to marking within the school. However, it is necessary for us to ask ourselves the questions:

1 Why are we marking the work?
2 Are we marking for our own sake or is it of value to the children?

Are we marking the work for neatness, tidiness, correct sentence structure and grammar, or are we marking for the scientific content? Does the record show that the pupil has understood what the Activity was all about? Does the record show that the child has learnt something from the Activity and is that 'something' that which we intended or is it some other aspect of the Activity which has caught the pupil's interest?

Should the marking include a numerical mark? If so, on what basis is the numerical mark awarded? Similarly, if a grade is given, how do we judge the grade for an individual child? Is the grade (or numerical mark) relative to that individual child's ability or is it a grade given to

that child's piece of work when compared with the same piece of work done by other members of the class?

Answers to these questions are not given here as the answers depend so much on the teacher and the school. But the raising of the questions for consideration is important.

The teacher's records

In the General Mastersheets published in conjunction with this book and the Pupils' Books, are two Mastersheets on which the teacher can keep a record of the Activities actually carried out by each member of the class. On Mastersheet G/1 there are spaces for twenty pupils and for all thirty-three Activities in Book 1A. On Mastersheet G/2 there are spaces for the names of twenty pupils and for the thirty-five Activities in Book 1B. The value to the class teacher of this record is that it shows exactly what has been done by all members of the class.

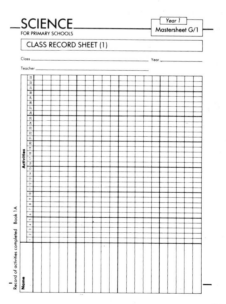

It also shows the teacher of the class next year if any areas of work (on which the Activities in Books 2A and 2B are based) have not been completed.

Mastersheet G/3 is a record sheet for individual members of the class. Besides recording the more general facts about the pupil, spaces are provided for recording comments about the pupil's general attitude to the work in science, his/her curiosity, ablity to work co-operatively with other pupils and general standard of recording (using criteria previously decided upon). Spaces are provided for the teacher to record other aspects of the child's progress.

One of the problems associated with a practical subject such as science is the provision and storage of the equipment needed to carry out the practical Activities.

At the end of this section a complete list is given of all the equipment needed to carry out the Activities in Books 1A and 1B. The equipment listed is that required for one group. From a perusal of this list it will be seen that much of the equipment merely needs collecting together – washing-up liquid bottles, plastic lemonade bottles, pots and jars, etc. Some items of equipment can be made if facilities are available and some items must be purchased. The cost of the equipment has been intentionally kept low.

As the apparatus is collected together it should be stored in labelled boxes. The labels should state the contents of the box and the Activity or Activities for which the contents are to be used. Thus, the box containing the balls used in the Activities in the Energy section of Book 1A could be labelled:

BALLS

12 table tennis
12 tennis
12 solid rubber
12 hollow plastic

BOOK 1A
ACTIVITIES 19, 20, 21

The storage of the equipment is very important. One area is needed in which all the science equipment is stored. This central store should be the responsibility of one member of staff who has a special interest in science. The equipment should not be used for purposes other than that for which it is intended. The balls for Book 1A provide a good example of the sort of equipment which, when there is a shortage of balls for a P.E. or games lesson, may be 'borrowed' with the promise that they will be returned as soon as the lesson is over. The promise will, of course, be made in good faith, but inevitably, some of the balls may get lost or mixed up with the P.E. balls. Some may not be returned, with the result that when a teacher wants to carry out these particular Activities the label on the box will be incorrect and the equipment no longer available. This can prove very irritating and frustrating as I know from personal experience.

The amount of storage space required for the equipment can be considerable, but the space must be found if the science course is to run smoothly in the school. The problem must be tackled and the solution found: it is not a problem which will just go away.

After equipment has been used and before it is returned to the central store, it should be cleaned and checked to see that it is in good condition. Any replacements should be obtained immediately.

The initial collection of the apparatus and its proper storage probably constitutes the biggest problem when organising a science course in a school. If this problem is solved, the science lessons should soon become an enjoyable experience for both teacher and pupils. This is particularly true when the items are consumable and therefore cannot be returned to the store. The substances used in the Water Activities in Book 1A need to be checked after use to see if there is sufficient remaining for the next time or whether a fresh supply must be obtained.

From the list of equipment it will be seen that plastic lemonade bottles are frequently needed. These can be collected from the children, but a direct approach to the parents either by letter or at a parents' meeting will result in a larger supply. The bottles have to be cut down for some of the Activities and this cutting must be done by the teacher or some other adult. The best way of cutting the bottles is to use a very sharp craft knife.

The items in this list are those required for *one group* to carry out the Activities in Pupils' Books 1A and 1B.

Activity	Item	Source
Time		
1	—	
2	centimetre-squared paper	Mastersheet G/4
3	—	
4	—	
5	—	
6	piece of chalk	school
7	clock or watch	suppliers 2, 3, 4, 5, 6
8	A4 paper	stationer
	plasticine	craft shop
	short stick or pencil	school or D.I.Y. shop
9	sticky tape	school
	jumping stand	school
	or box of stones and stick	garden centre
10	chalk	school
	or paint	D.I.Y. shop
	wood 30 × 2.5 × 5cm	D.I.Y. shop
	plasticine	craft shop
	short stick about 15cm long	D.I.Y. shop
Water		
11	sugar cubes (quick dissolving)	grocer
12	jar	home
	jars	home
	spoon or rod (stirring)	home
	spoon for measuring	home
	substances:	grocer, chemist
	cooking salt	
	icing sugar	
	flour	
	washing soda	
	bicarbonate of soda	
	Epsom salts	
	Glauber's salt	

Activity	Item	Source
Ourselves		
24	feelie box (see construction notes)	supplier 1 or school
25	envelopes of things to feel	see later notes
	sets of smelling jars (see later notes)	home, chemist
26	things to taste e.g. icing sugar, salt, flour, vinegar, bitter lemon sweets	see later notes
27	Mystery Boxes (see construction notes)	school
28	cards	school
	long measuring tape	school
	or click wheel	school
Structures		
29	A4 duplicating paper	stationer
30	A4 duplicating paper	stationer
	card 15cm square	stationer
	yoghurt pot or similar	home
	marbles	toy shop, supplier 1
31	as 29	
32	30cm wooden rod (dowel) 25-35mm thick	D.I.Y. shop
	30cm wooden rod 12-15mm thick	
	sticky tape	school
	yoghurt pot with hanging string	home
	marbles	toy shop, supplier 1
	books or wooden blocks or support stands	school
	(see construction notes)	supplier 1
33	22 sheets from same newspaper	home
	sticky tape	school
	bathroom scales	home or department store

No.	Equipment	Source
13	jars	home
	spoon or rod (stirring)	home
	liquids to test:	grocer
	cooking oil	
	vinegar	
	syrup	
	washing-up liquid	
	milk	
14	piece of chalk	school
15	plastic lemonade bottle	home
	sticky paper	school
16	jar with screw top	home
	dish	home
17	ice cubes	school or home
	(1) jars and dishes	school or home
	measuring jug	home
	(2) 2 bottles – 1 stoppered	department store
18	dropper	home
	cloth 15cm square	chemist
		home

Energy 1

No.	Equipment	Source
19	4 different balls	toy shop
	metre stick	suppliers 1, 2, 3, 4, 5, 6
	(see construction notes)	
20	plasticine	craft shop
	balls from 19	
	metre stick	suppliers 1, 2, 3, 4, 5, 6
	plasticine	craft shop
	square of carpet	home
	square of plastic foam	home or department store
21	square of hardboard	D.I.Y. shop
	cotton wool	chemist
	balls from 19	
	board 1 metre long × 15cm wide	D.I.Y. shop
	(see construction notes)	
	plasticine	craft shop
	measuring tape	Mastersheet G/5
22	books or wooden blocks	school or D.I.Y. shop
	model car	toy shop
23	slope and tape as in 21 as 22	

Air

No.	Equipment	Source
34	thin stick 30cm long	garden centre, D.I.Y. shop
		stationer
	2 paper clips	craft shop
	2 beads	toy shop
35	balloon	suppliers 2, 3, 4, 5, 6
36	plastic aquarium	home, department store
	clear plastic jar	
37	as 36 with 1 more plastic jar	home
	bottle	chemist
38	funnel	craft shop, stationer
	plasticine or Blu-tack	stationer
	wire about 10cm long (straightened paper clip)	
39	bottle	home
	drinking straw (plastic)	department store
	plasticine	craft shop
40	plastic washing-up liquid bottle	home
	50cm plastic tubing	wine-makers' shop, iron-monger's shop

Animals

No.	Equipment	Source
41	box with damp soil (margarine box with lid)	home, school
	garden fork (hand)	
42	large glass or plastic jar or wormery (see construction notes)	garden centre, department store
	black paper	sweet shop
	sand	supplier 1
	soil	
43	wormery as 42	stationer
	potato, carrot, swede	garden centre
	green leaves, dead leaves	garden, field, etc.
44	blotting paper	greengrocer
	cotton wool	garden
	peppermint flavouring	stationer
		chemist
45	hand lens	department store, grocer
	sheet of A4 paper	suppliers 1-6
		stationer

Activity	Item	Source
46	box with damp soil (as 41)	
47	plastic box	suppliers 2-6
	or plastic aquarium	
	small stones	garden, field, etc.
	damp soil	
	small tufts of grass	
48	paper	stationer
	clear plastic	D.I.Y. shop (clear
		acrylic sheet used
		for double glazing)
		or supplier 1
49	clear plastic as 48	
	flour and water paste	
50	lettuce, grass, potato,	home, garden
	apple, sugar	
51	orange skin	greengrocer
	torch	department store
	2 spoons	home, department store
	blunt pencil	school
52	—	
53	2 plastic drinking cups or	department store,
	yoghurt pots	home
	string	school, department store
	2 dead matchsticks	
	1 plastic drinking cup	department store
	1 dead matchstick	
	string (for extension)	
54	model stethoscope made	
	from:	
	plastic tubing	pet shop which
	Y piece	sells aquarium
		accessories
	3 plastic funnels	department store,
	(see construction notes)	chemist, iron monger
55	—	
56	A4 paper	stationer
	glue	school
	scissors	school

Activity	Item	Source
Plants		
57	leaf from tree	park (check with
		keeper), field
58	leaf from tree	park (check with
		keeper), field
		Mastersheet G/4
59	cm squared paper	chemist
	plaster of Paris	department store
	mixing bowl	home, department store
	spoon	
	plasticine	craft shop
	leaf	park, field
60	paints and brushes	school
	A4 paper	stationer
	crayons	craft shop
	or heel ball	shoe repair shop
	sticky tape	school
61	string	department store
	measuring tape	Mastersheet G/5
62	stick about 30cm long	garden centre, D.I.Y. shop
63	measuring tape	Mastersheet G/5
64	—	
Light and colour		
65	torch	department store
66	screen (cardboard)	stationer
	torch (as 65)	
	sheet of white paper (A3)	stationer
	pencil	stationer
67	shadow theatre	supplier 1
	(or see constructional notes)	
	card	stationer
	glue	school
	scissors	school
68	mirror	supplier 1
	(see construction notes)	
	torch (as 65)	
69	torch (as 65)	
	2 mirrors (see 68)	supplier 1
	card screen (as 65)	

ACTIVITIES
Book 1A

TIME

Introduction

Time has been selected as one of the ten themes in the Pupils' Books because the development of the concept of time is very important to pupils. Also it provides some excellent material for investigative science.

The concept of time is difficult to define or describe. A child may be able to 'tell the time' from the position of the hands on a clockface, but this does not necessarily mean that he or she has any mental idea of a second, a minute or an hour. The concept of time involves a mental understanding of the units of time measurement: from the second to the week, month and year. It also involves an understanding of our position in the time continuum. We are in the here and now, with the past behind us and the future in front of us. As part of the process of developing a concept of time, children will gather a vocabulary of time words: today, tomorrow, yesterday, week, month, year, summer, winter and so on. However, we should bear in mind that young children frequently use time words without necessarily having a concept of time.

Lovell, in his book *The Growth of Mathematical and Scientific Concepts in Children* (University of London Press, 5th edition 1966), states that when children are developing a concept of time 'it is probable that watching or listening to an activity that has a clear beginning and ending is likely to be a learning situation, as far as the time concept is concerned'. So, throughout the four years covered by the Pupils' Books, the Activities will provide opportunities for the pupils to be involved in many happenings which have a clear beginning and ending.

In the first year a start is made by looking at the time as displayed by ordinary clockfaces and digital clockfaces. The digital watch is now commonplace and it is useful for the children to be able to 'tell the time' from both types of watch and to realise, for example, that a digital watch displaying '4.29' is showing the same time as a watch with hands showing 'nearly half past four'.

This is followed by an Activity concerned with the children's birthdays. The next Activity is about the way we break down the year into the four seasons, winter, spring, summer and autumn. This section will probably be tackled at the beginning of the school year in September. The work can be linked with, perhaps, art and craft and poetry.

Activity 4 is designed to get the children thinking about the way their day is divided into time periods.

The remainder of the section on time deals with the ideas behind the sundial.

Activity 1   CLOCKS AND WATCHES

Aim
To check whether the children can tell the time. For the children to relate the time displayed by the hands of an ordinary watch to the time displayed by a digital watch.

Mastersheet
Each child will require a copy of Mastersheet 1 and Mastersheet 2.

Activity
The Activity begins with a discussion about the drawings on page 4. (The children should, perhaps, be warned not to draw in the book). Some children in the class may have watches. Many of these will be of the digital type, whereas the clocks around the school will almost certainly be those with hands and figures.

The discussion should lead to a realisation that, for example, 'a quarter past ten' is the same as 10.15 or that 11.20 is the same as 'twenty past eleven'.

Mastersheet 1 shows digital watches displaying the time. The clock faces opposite have no hands. The children draw in the hands to show the same times as the digital watches.

Conversely, Mastersheet 2 has clock faces with hands showing the time. The children have to put the appropriate time on the digital watches.

More able children will complete this Activity fairly quickly. However, it may reveal to the

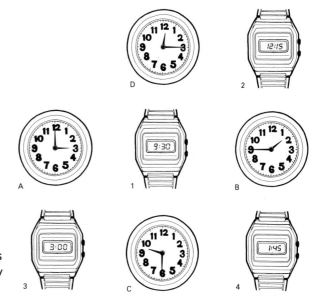

teacher that some of the children cannot tell the time and that others do not realise that 4.15 is the same as 'a quarter past four'. The appropriate corrective measures can then be applied.

Follow-up
Throughout this section the children can be on the lookout for pictures of watches, clocks and other time-keeping instruments to put in their folders or notebooks. A frieze or collage about time-keeping always promotes a great deal of interest.

Activity 2   BIRTHDAYS

Aim
To give the children experience in collecting simple statistical data.
For the children to use the collected data:
(a) to provide further information

(b) to draw a simple bar graph (histogram) from which other information can be derived.
To get the children thinking about the length of time in a year.
To provide practice in counting.

Mastersheet

Mastersheet 3 has the months of the year down the left hand side with a space next to each month. This is for marking in the number of children whose birthdays fall in that month. The column on the right is for the total for each month. The total at the bottom of this column is the number of children in the class.

Mastersheet G/4 is centimetre-squared paper. This is for the histogram: the months are plotted along the horizontal axis and the number of birthdays up the vertical axis.

Activity

Birthdays are important days for children and the Activity could begin with a discussion about birthdays and how we celebrate them. The children then use the Mastersheet to collect their data. After this they answer the questions in the middle of page 5. Finally, the bar graph can be drawn. If the children have not made a graph before, this will be a good opportunity to introduce them to the technique. The children should be reminded to label both the horizontal ('Month') and vertical ('Number of birthdays') axes and to give the graph a title.

Recording

The Mastersheet and the graph will provide suitable records for this Activity. The children could write a few sentences describing what they did and what they found out.

Follow-up

One interesting area which could be investigated here is the length of life of various animals.

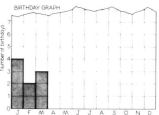

Activity 2   BIRTHDAYS

You will need
Mastersheet 3
centimetre squared
paper

When is your birthday?
Find out the month in which each child in your class has his or her birthday.

Write the number of birthdays in each month on your Mastersheet like this:

Month	Number of birthdays	Total
January	/ / / /	4
February	/ /	2

In which month are there most birthdays?
In which month are there the smallest number of birthdays?
Are there any months when nobody has a birthday?
Make a bar graph to show the number of birthdays in each month.
Use the centimetre squared paper.
Start like this:

BIRTHDAY GRAPH

Here are some examples of life expectancies:

mayfly 1 day	lion 25 years
mouse 2-3 years	horse 30 years
rabbit 12 years	elephant 60 years
cat 12-16 years	tortoise 100 years
owl 24 years	

This material could be used to construct another bar graph which would make an interesting wall display with illustrations.

Activity 3   THE SEASONS

Aim

To show that one way of dividing the year is by the naturally occurring seasons.

Mastersheet

Each pupil will need a copy of Mastersheet 4.

Activity

A start can be made by discussing with the children what part or season of the year we are in now. This can be followed by a discussion on what season will inevitably follow. The other two seasons which bring us back to the present season can then be talked about. The children could be asked what sort of things happen in each season.

On Mastersheet 4 the children draw pictures to illustrate the four seasons. Under each picture the months for each season should be written:

Autumn   September, October, part November
Winter   part November, December, January, February
Spring   March, April, May
Summer   June, July, August

The seasons can, of course, vary depending on the weather.

Recording

Mastersheet 4 should provide sufficient record for this Activity.

Follow-up

With classes in which there are pupils who have lived abroad, an interesting discussion can follow on the weather and seasons in other countries. An American boy in one of my classes surprised us all by describing the heavy snowfall they get in the State of Texas! This was followed by an account of how he and his mother had seen a rattlesnake sleeping in the very hot sun in the summer. Australian children tell of celebrating Christmas in midsummer. In some countries such as Brazil, there is no autumn and the leaves do not fall from the trees as they do in this country.

A frieze showing the four seasons can be made by the whole class. One teacher divided her class into four groups, one for each season. Each group then made a large collage/picture. The pictures were joined in the correct order to make a large circle. Sitting inside the circle the children could look round and see how the seasons change.

Activity 4   SCHOOL TIME

Aim

To focus the children's attention on the fact that their day is divided up into periods of time and on how the school day is largely ruled by the clock.

Equipment

Each child will need a copy of Mastersheet 5.

Mastersheet

Mastersheet 5 has a series of clock faces down the left hand side with spaces next to them. The clock faces have no hands marked.

Activity

The two photographs on page 7 show children at school at two different times of the day. In the first picture the children are working in a classroom and in the second picture the children

SCIENCE
FOR PRIMARY SCHOOLS

Year 1
Mastersheet 5

Name_____ Date_____

SCHOOL TIME

Time	What happens

are playing in the playground. Playtime is a particular part of the school day. We look at the clock to find out when to go into the playground for playtime.

The Mastersheet can be used in one of two ways:

1 Throughout a school day the children fill in the times when they do specific things: start of school, when they do number work, playtime and so on.

2 With help from the teacher it can be filled in at one time. In this case the teacher will have to tell the children the various times.

Recording

The Mastersheet itself will provide sufficient record. A short note might be added by the children saying how the days of the week differ. For example, it might happen that they have painting on Monday afternoon, or on Wednesday morning they have games.

Activity 5   LOOKING AT YOUR SHADOW

Aim

For the children to look at shadows and to see the relationship between the source of the light (the Sun), themselves and the shadows that they cast.

Equipment

None

Safety Note

It is absolutely essential to impress upon the children the danger of looking directly at the Sun. This warning is printed in the Pupils' Book, but the warning must also be given verbally to cover those children who cannot or do not read this warning.

Activity

As stated in the Pupils' Book, the essential requirement for this Activity is a bright, sunny day when good clear shadows are cast. When the children are in the playground, they should spread out so that they can see their own shadow clearly. Before going into the playground the children should read page 8. On returning to the classroom, the position of the Sun and the shadow can be discussed.

Recording

Most children will need some help with the drawings. Matchstick men are quite easily

TIME

Activity 5   LOOKING AT YOUR SHADOW

You will need
a sunny day

Go into the playground when your teacher tells you to.
Look at your shadow.
Find out where your shadow is when:

1 the Sun is in front of you
2 the Sun is behind you
3 the Sun is to your left
4 the Sun is to your right.

WARNING!
Do not look at the Sun.
It can hurt your eyes.

In your notebook draw 4 pictures.
Each picture should show: you, the Sun, your shadow.

● Can you see your shadow if it is a cloudy day?

page 8

drawn and will make it easier for the children to draw the shadows.

The question 'What happens if it is a cloudy day?' is intended to bring out the fact that the Sun is still shining, but that the shadows (if any) are not clear. The sunlight has been scattered by the clouds.

Activity 6   SHADOWS

Aim

For the children to see that shadows move and change shape with the passage of time. Incidentally, this Activity will also give children the experience of what twenty minutes is like.

Equipment

Each pair of children will need a piece of chalk.

Activity

The safety warning about not looking at the Sun should be repeated by the teacher in case any children were absent when the previous warning was given. When in the playground, the children should be told to space themselves out so that their shadows do not overlap. If the size of the playground is such that this is not possible, the children can be given coloured chalk to help distinguish the shadows.

    It is very important in this Activity that the children stand in *exactly* the same place where their shoes were drawn round. I find that the children will try to move around to match their shadow with the previously drawn outline. After twenty minutes there should be a considerable movement of the shadow.

Recording

The children could draw pictures to show the difference in the shadows after twenty minutes.

A few sentences would help to show whether the children understand what they have found out.

    As a class display the shadows of one pupil as seen twenty minutes apart could be drawn on some large sheets of light-coloured sugar paper which have been joined together.

Activity 7   WHERE IS THE SUN?

Aim

To bring to the children's attention the apparent movement of the Sun across the sky. This is in preparation for the following Activities on sundials.

Mastersheet

Each child will need a copy of Mastersheet 6.

Special note

This Activity is very important and gives the children an understanding of simple sundials. The Activity does, however, pose a difficult problem. If we are not careful we will leave the children with the idea that the Sun rises in the East, moves across the sky and then sets in the West. This is what we see, but our initial interpretation of the observed facts is, as we well know, wrong. It is the movement of the Earth itself in relation to the Sun which causes the movement of the shadows, etc.

Now, as teachers of these young children, we have to decide what to do. Two paths are open to us:

1 After the Activity has been completed we could discuss with the children what they have discovered. From their observations we could lead toward a general conclusion that the Sun seems to rise in the East and move across the sky. Then we could emphasise that there is another explanation of this apparent motion. Some children may volunteer statements such as 'the Earth is round' or 'the Earth is spinning round'. We can quickly outline the Earth – Sun relationship, but not push it too hard. This is an extremely difficult concept for children of this age.

2 After the Activity we could discuss what the children have discovered and use the opportunity to
   (a) outline the fact that the Earth is ball-shaped. Photographs taken from space are very useful here.
   (b) explain that the Earth is spinning round

like a top and that it takes 24 hours to spin round once.
   (c) explain that as the Earth is spinning and the Sun is stationary, it means that while one part of the Earth is illuminated by the Sun (day-time) another part of the Earth is away from the Sun and is dark (night-time).
   (d) these facts can all be shown with a model. A table lamp (be careful, the bulb gets very hot!) can be used to represent the Sun and a ball can represent the Earth. If the ball is now held a metre or so away from the lamp, the children will be able to see that the part of the ball away from the lamp is not illuminated. The side of the ball nearest the lamp is brightly illuminated and this represents the part of the Earth in day-time. If a mark is made on the ball and the ball turned while being held up near the lamp the children can see how the mark moves through 'day-time' and into the 'night'.

The choice of which path to take must depend on the teacher and the teacher's judgement of the ability of the class to understand this difficult concept.

Activity 8   MAKING A SHADOW CLOCK

Aim

To use the knowledge gained from the previous Activities to make a simple shadow clock or sundial. This involves the children in measuring fifteen minute time intervals and in making a series of observations.

Special note

After the sundial has been set up, the Activity involves about two minutes work in every fifteen minutes. It is best if the Activity is continued over at least two hours, longer if possible. This does mean, however, that the children should have other work to do when they are making their observations. You could, for example, carry out

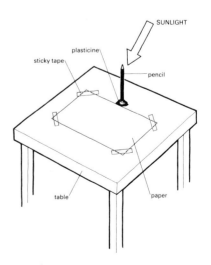

Activities 1 and 2 during this time, instead of at the beginning.

Equipment

The short stick or pencil used in this Activity should not be longer than about ten centimetres. The other essential is a sunny part of the classroom. When the children are working in groups it is difficult to find sufficient space in an ordinary classroom. One answer to this problem is to work in the playground or the school hall or along corridors. It is worthwhile looking round the school to find suitable places.

The sheet of paper should be A4 size or larger. On A4 paper the shadow of a ten centimetre stick may well fall over the edge of the paper, particularly in winter.

Activity

It is advisable to discuss the Activity with the class the previous afternoon so that they will be ready to start first thing in the morning. The best places for fixing the sheet of paper and the way to draw round the shadow and put on the time can be demonstrated.

The next morning, if it is sunny, the children can tape (or use Blu-tack) the paper to the table top. The plasticine is used to hold the stick upright in the middle of the long side nearest to the Sun. At the start the first shadow is drawn round and marked with the time. After each quarter of an hour this is repeated. A kitchen timer set to ring after fifteen minutes has been found useful here.

Recording

The children could record this Activity by describing in words and pictures what they did and what they found out.

Follow-up

On the next sunny day the sundial can be checked to see if it tells the time correctly.

If the children can use a centimetre rule (Mastersheet G/6) they could measure the length of the shadow every fifteen minutes and then draw a simple graph to show how the length alters with time during the day. Another method of making the graph is to actually cut out (or trace off) the marked shadows. These can then be mounted in order on a sheet of centimetre-squared paper (Mastersheet G/4).

Activity 9   A PLAYGROUND SUNDIAL

Aim

To consolidate and reinforce Activity 8 and to involve the children in a corporate Activity. This Activity also gives the children experience of half-hour intervals.

Equipment

If the sundial is to be reasonably permanent, then a broom handle which has been given two or three coats of polyurethane varnish should be used as the gnomon (shadow stick). The broom handle should be firmly hammered into the ground or supported in a plastic bucket or large tin of stones. If the sundial is to be used over a period of a few weeks, a jumping stand could be used, provided it is firmly wedged in place.

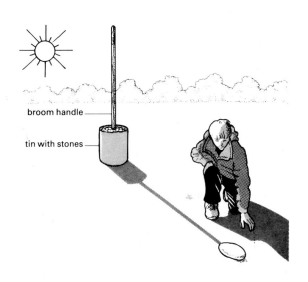

broom handle

tin with stones

The half-hour marks can either be chalked or painted on the playground. If the sundial is being made on the field, housebricks can be placed at the end of the shadows. The times could be painted on the bricks.

Activity

Preparations for the calibration of the sundial should be made on the previous day at least. Discussions can take place as to where the sundial should be sited and the gnomon fixed in place. The bricks needed for the time marks can be painted. A roster can be prepared so that at the end of each half-hour throughout the day two children go out and mark in the time on the sundial.

As this is a special event for the children, perhaps a start could be made at, say, half past eight in the morning and it could continue for an hour after school normally finishes.

A permanent sundial can be made by burying the bricks so that the tops are level with the ground.

Recording

The children could write about what they did and illustrate their record with a drawing of the finished sundial.

Follow-up

The children could be encouraged to look for sundials in gardens, on old churches and so on. It is surprising how many sundials there are: some sundials are works of art. The collection of various types of sundials in the Science Museum at South Kensington, London, is well worth a visit.

Activity 10   MAKING AN EGYPTIAN SUNBAR

Aim

To find out if shadows decrease in length up to noon, and increase in length after noon.
To relate the variation in shadow length to the apparent motion of the Sun.

Equipment

Strips of thick card or hardboard work well, but wood with the dimensions specified in the Pupils' Book and Equipment List is best. Supplier 1 will provide these models already made up and painted ready to be calibrated. If the calibrations are made with a felt-tip pen they can be rubbed off with a damp cloth after use.

Activity

The plasticine is pushed on to one end of the strip. The pencil or stick is pushed into the plasticine so that it is at right angles to the long strip of wood. The children should take their sunbars out of the classroom and point the end with the pencil or stick towards the Sun. The position of the shadow and the time should be

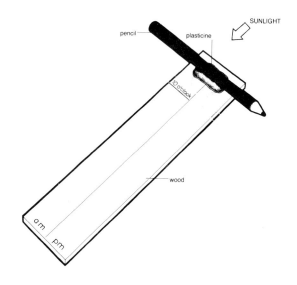

marked on the strip. Half-hour intervals are suitable. Morning times should be marked down one side of the bar and afternoon times down the other side.

Special note

These simple sunbars are apparently still used in parts of North Africa. They are used for timing periods of irrigation in the fields.

Recording

The children could describe how they made and calibrated the sunbars, illustrating their writing with pictures.

Mastersheet

Mastersheet 7 shows how to make a simple ring sundial. The long strip is cut out and the hole made at the points shown. The strip is then joined end to end to make a ring. A short length of string is threaded through the pair of holes and tied to make a loop. The other marked hole is best cut with a punch to give a sharp edge.

To calibrate the ring sundial, it should be suspended from the index finger and the hole directed towards the Sun. When the sundial is properly aligned the beam of light will hit the inner side of the circle which will be in shade. The position of the beam of light should be marked with the time: half-hour intervals are suitable. The calibratoin should be done while the children are working in pairs, but each child can make a sundial. After calibration and checking, the sundials can be taken home by the children. I have found that they are generally received with considerable interest by parents.

WATER

Introduction

This section provides an introduction to one of the most important and interesting properties of water: its ability to dissolve many substances. The aim of the four sections on water in Books 1A, 2A, 3A and 4A is to provide a practical basis for an understanding of the water cycle on which all forms of life depend.

It is important to realise just how complicated and difficult it is to understand the water cycle. Some of the concepts involved are too difficult for the majority of primary school children to comprehend, but this does not mean to say that we should ignore a concept just because it is difficult. We should try to find practical ways of introducing these ideas at a level which is understandable to the children at their particular stage of development.

For example, the processes of dissolving and evaporation are very complicated. To get any deep understanding of them a knowledge of the behaviour of atoms and molecules is needed. However, these complicated and important processes can be introduced to children of this age in a simple, direct, practical manner. Evaporation can be introduced by a consideration of washing drying on a clothes line. This approach will provide the children with a good practical basis for the more theoretical work which follows at secondary level. Incidentally, this approach can provide us with some good scientific activities.

The first part of the section introduces the idea of dissolving. This is followed by a look at evaporation, leading to the question 'Where has the water gone?'. The final part introduces the process of condensation. Condensation is important here. If this process is not introduced at this stage, the children might be left with the idea that when water evaporates it disappears, never to be seen again. Even at this early stage, one of the basic laws of science, 'matter can neither be created nor destroyed', can be obliquely, if not directly, introduced.

On page 14 there are four drawings showing common uses of water: washing, watering the garden, cooking and drinking. These provide an introduction to Mastersheet 8. On Mastersheet 8 there are a number of clockfaces down the left-hand side and a space opposite each clockface. Throughout one day, the children record how they use water at certain times which they mark on the clockfaces. There are not sufficient spaces for *all* the times when the children use water (toilet, washing, painting, drinking, etc) but writing down when and how water is used focuses their attention on the fact that we are dependent on water for the smooth running of our lives. Discussion of this with the children could include the ideas that without water we would die, and that any shortage of water causes, at least, great inconvenience.

_SCIENCE_____
FOR PRIMARY SCHOOLS

| Year 1 |
| Mastersheet 8 |

Name_____ Date_____

| USING WATER |

Time	How I used water
🕐	
🕐	
🕐	
🕐	
🕐	
🕐	

On the day before the Mastersheet is used, a discussion with the class could emphasise that considerable quantities of water are used when, for example, the toilet is flushed, or our clothes are washed, or many of our foods are cooked. A cup of tea or coffee could not be made without water, neither could a loaf of bread or an apple pie.

Activity 11   A SUGAR CUBE IN WATER

Aim

To give the children an opportunity for careful observation and to provide an introduction to the idea of dissolving.

Equipment

For this Activity a clear glass or plastic container containing warm (not hot) water is needed. As most classrooms are not equipped with a supply of hot water, I have found it convenient to take to the classroom a kettle from the staff room. For those classrooms not fitted with a sink, it is advisable to have buckets available in which the waste water can be collected for disposal later.

Mastersheet

Each pupil will require a copy of Mastersheet 9.

Special note

In general terms, the hotter the water the quicker the cube will dissolve. In most supermarkets quick-dissolving sugar cubes can be purchased. These dissolve in about 4 minutes at about 25°C.

It is important that the children understand that they should not stir the water nor move the jar once the cube has been added. We want the children to see the process of dissolving taking place: we do not want to complicate the situation by moving the water around.

Activity

Ideally, each child should have a jar of warm water and a sugar cube. At a given signal from the teacher, the cubes are placed in the water. Drawings are then made (Mastersheet 9) to show the sequence of events.

As a variation on this Activity, I have found that the use of a stopclock adds interest. The stopclock is started as the cubes are placed in the water. The drawings are then made at 1 minute, 2 minutes and 6 minutes. The last drawing is easy to complete – the cube has dissolved by this time.

Recording

It is very important that the children draw what they see. This Activity is an exercise in observation. In the second drawing the children will probably put in dots to represent the bubbles of air which come from the cube. This air is trapped in the cube between the sugar crystals as the cube is made.

The Mastersheet, when completed, provides a suitable record of this Activity, although the children might also write a few short notes about what happened.

Follow-up

When we ask the children 'What has happened to the sugar cube?', they will usually give one of three answers:

1 it has melted
2 it has disappeared
3 it has dissolved.

Of these three, only the last is correct.

Melting is a completely different process from dissolving and it is important to clarify this point. A lump of ice at room temperature absorbs heat energy and changes into the liquid state. A lump of sugar will also melt if it is heated. Melting is a change from the solid to the liquid state. Dissolving is the mixing of one substance with another. The particles of the dissolved substance are extremely small (molecular size or smaller) and spread out among the particles of the other substance. The resulting solution is clear because the separated particles are too small to be seen. Heat *may* be involved in the process of dissolving, but it is *always* involved in the process of melting.

The sugar cube is no longer visible at the end of the Activity but we should carefully check that the children realise that the sugar has not vanished. It is still there even though it can no longer be seen. The children can dip their (clean) fingers into the solution and check by taste the presence of the sugar.

Before leaving this Activity we can point out to the children the properties of a (water) solution:

1 it is clear – light can pass through the solution
2 particles of the dissolved substance cannot be seen in the solution.

Activity 12   WHAT DISSOLVES IN WATER?

Aim

To give the children practice in recognising a solution and to show that some substances do not (apparently) dissolve in water. Incidentally, this Activity will also give the children experience in organising their work and recording.

Equipment

The clear plastic drinking cups available from many shops are very suitable for this Activity. Glass jars of the type used for baby foods are also very good. Plastic teaspoons are quite cheap but wooden stirring rods are available (Supplier 1) or see the construction notes.

Mastersheet

Each child will require a copy of Mastersheet 10.

Activity

The substances for testing could include:

cooking salt	chalk (powder)
granulated sugar	Epsom salts
icing sugar	bicarbonate of soda
instant coffee	flour
washing powder	cornflour
soda crystals (care)	baking powder
toothpaste	

The substances should be kept in small labelled jars and each jar should have its own spoon. The jars should be placed in a central part of the classroom.

To test each substance, the plastic cup is about half filled with water (warm or cold). One small spoonful of the substance to be tested is added. The name of the substance is written in the appropriate column on Mastersheet 10. The mixture is stirred with the stirring rod or plastic spoon. The mixture is left for a few minutes. The children then decide if the substance has dissolved or not. If it has, a tick is put in the 'Dissolves' column of the Mastersheet. If it has not dissolved, a tick is put in the 'Does not dissolve' column.

After each substance has been tested, the contents of the jar should be emptied down the sink (or poured into the bucket). The jar and spoon should be washed in the sink or a bowl of water. If paper towels are available the spoon and the jar should be dried before the next substance is tested.

Follow-up

Once the Activity has been completed, the classroom tidied up and the equipment put away, the children's findings can be discussed.

The flour mixes with the water, but on leaving the mixture for a while, the flour can be seen settling in a layer at the bottom of the jar and the water is misty. The mistiness is caused by very small particles of flour in the water. Flour, then, does not appear to dissolve in water. We should be careful here. To be absolutely correct (and scientific) we should say that, as far as we can see, the flour does not dissolve in water. We have no way of finding out if a small part of the flour has dissolved. How far the teacher takes this sort of discussion will depend on the teacher and the ability of the class. Many teachers may prefer to leave the results clear-cut as 'dissolves' and 'does not dissolve'.

If time allows, the teacher could demonstrate to the children the effect of using hot water. Washing powder and instant coffee dissolve much more rapidly.

Activity 13   DO LIQUIDS DISSOLVE IN WATER?

Aim

To look at another type of solution: the liquid-in-liquid solution.

Equipment

The liquids for this Activity can include any that are found in the average home or school, providing they are safe for the children to use. Examples are: washing-up liquid, cooking oil, milk, vinegar, syrup (golden), glycerine.

Besides the equipment used in the previous Activity, a tablespoon for measuring the liquids is needed.

Mastersheet

Each child will require a copy of Mastersheet 11.

Activity

Two tablespoonfuls of each of the liquids are added to a jar about half full of water. The mixture is then stirred quite vigorously. The mixture should be left for a few minutes before a decision is made as to whether the liquid has dissolved in the water or not.

The washing-up liquid, glycerine and syrup do dissolve but quite slowly. The cooking oil does not dissolve: it separates out and floats on top of the water. Milk is interesting as it is not possible to give a definite answer to whether it dissolves or not. The milk certainly mixes with the water, but the water is not clear and does not conform to the rule set out above for a solution. But perhaps a part of the milk has dissolved in the water and a part has not. This, in fact, is correct, but in the classroom situation we cannot say with absolute certainty that this is the case. The vinegar, if it is the brown variety, does dissolve in the water and it is interesting to see how the brown colour is evenly diluted as it mixes with the water.

From their results on the Mastersheet, the children will be able to see that some liquids do dissolve in water, some do not and others, apparently, partly dissolve.

The children could try other liquids.

Activity 14   WHERE DOES A PUDDLE GO?

Aim

To provide an introduction to the process of evaporation. The children will already know about evaporation in a very general way. Now we plan to bring the process of evaporation to their direct attention.

Equipment

As Pupils' Book.

Activity

The best sort of weather for this Activity is a very warm, breezy day. The amount of water used should be quite small, say between 100 and 150cm³. Of course, if a shower of rain is followed by bright, warm sunshine, the naturally formed puddles can be used. After the children have made the puddles, they draw round them with chalk. The line should be just outside the puddle so that the chalk is not washed away. After some time, dependent on the prevailing weather conditions, the puddle should be drawn round again. This can be repeated until the puddle 'disappears'.

Recording

The children could make some simple drawings in their notebook to show what they did, and write a few short sentences to explain what they found out.

Follow-up

The Activity should make the children think about the process of evaporation, by which water changes from a liquid to a vapour. This vapour is invisible, but is, nevertheless, present in the air. Discussion with the children can centre round the fact that the water from the puddle and from the washing on the drier cannot just disappear – it must be somewhere. The class can also think about the best weather for drying clothes. What happens to the water on our skin when we come out of the swimming pool?

Activity 15   WATCHING WATER DRY UP

Aim

To allow the children to observe the evaporation of water over a longer period of time and in a more quantitative way.
To reinforce the idea of evaporation.

Equipment

The plastic lemonade bottles are best cut while the labels are still on them: the labels provide a straight cutting line. The height of the bottles for this Activity should be about 15-20cm. The strip of sticky paper should be about 3cm wide.

Activity

The bottle is filled to a point about 2cm from the top, after the paper strip has been stuck on. The water level is marked with a line. (Note: for accuracy the water level should be viewed by bending down so that the eyes are level with the top of the water.) The line should be marked with the date. The bottles are then placed in a warm part of the classroom. The water levels should be marked each day at the same time.

Follow-up

Discussion could centre on the fact that the water has evaporated and the question of where the water has gone. If there are noticeable differences in the amounts of water which have evaporated on different days, it might be possible to consider why the differences have occurred.

Activity 16   WHERE DOES THE WATER GO?

Note: this Activity should be carried out as a demonstration by the teacher.

Aim

To show the children that there is water vapour in the air and that we can condense this water vapour on to a cold surface.

Equipment

A fairly large jar with a screw top and a supply of ice cubes are needed. Ideally the ice cubes should fill the jar, but if this is not possible, the jar can be topped up with cold water. The jar should stand in a deep plate or soup dish.

Activity

The jar is filled with ice cubes. The lid is screwed on the jar and the outside of the jar dried. It is then placed in the dish and the children watch to see what happens. The very cold surface of the jar soon becomes 'misted up' and soon after drops of water run down the outside of the jar and collect in the dish. As these things happen, they should be discussed with the class:

What do you think the liquid is? (It should *not* be tasted.)
Where has the liquid come from?
Could it have leaked out from the jar?

Recording

The children could make their own drawings of the apparatus and then write a few sentences describing what happened. Finally, they should be encouraged to explain what they saw happening.

Follow-up

The similarity between what the children saw in this Activity and what happens in the kitchen or bathroom could be discussed. The formation of clouds by the condensation of water vapour could also be discussed.

Activity 17   WATER EVAPORATING 1

Aim

To provide a practical basis for the discussion of evaporation.
To allow the children to think about evaporation and to predict from their observations what they think will occur.

Equipment

Various jars and dishes are needed. A jam jar, a drinking cup, a soup dish, a basin are examples.

Activity

The measuring jug is used to pour the same amount of water into each container. The water level is marked on each container.

A 'permanent' marker pen should be used to mark the water level. An ordinary felt-tip pen is not suitable.

The children should be asked what they think is going to happen to the water in the containers if they are left for a few days in the same part of the classroom. Then they could be asked if they think the water will evaporate more quickly from some of the containers. If so, then from which container will the water evaporate most quickly and why?

After a few days (4-5) the water levels are marked again. The volumes of water remaining in the containers could be measured: this gives a direct measurement of the amounts of water which have evaporated from the different containers.

Recording

Simple drawings of the before and after type could be made by the children in their notebooks. If the volumes of the water have been measured at the beginning and the end of the Activity, these volumes could be included in their drawings.

The children could write about their predictions and whether they were correct or not.

Activity 17   WATER EVAPORATING 2

Aim

To finalise these preliminary ideas about evaporation. What is going to happen in this Activity should be obvious to the children by now.

Equipment

Two plastic lemonade bottles or similar are needed. Another, smaller bottle or a measuring jug is required to measure the same volume of water into each of the two bottles.

Activity

The children put the same volume of water in both bottles. One bottle is then stoppered and the other left unstoppered. The children should be asked to say what they think is going to happen to the water. Will it evaporate from both bottles? If not, why not? If the bottles are left in a warm place, will the water evaporate quickly from the unstoppered bottle? The water levels in the two bottles are marked and they are placed in a warm place. The water levels are checked after a few days. One pair of bottles could be left for a much longer time and the rate of evaporation

noted. As the plastic lemonade bottle has a narrow neck, the rate of evaporation is quite slow, even when the stopper is left off.

Recording

A drawing of the two bottles with the water levels marked could be accompanied by a few short sentences describing what the children did and what they found out.

When the children make their first recording, they could write down what they think is going to happen and why. Later on they could say whether their predictions were correct.

Activity 18   DRYING A WET CLOTH

Aim

To use the children's knowledge of evaporation in a scientific test.
To revise and consolidate the idea of scientific testing.

Equipment

For the initial test 3 squares (each 15cm square) of the same cloth are needed. If the test is carried further as suggested at the bottom of page 23, squares of other sorts of cloth will be needed. To provide a good contrast in drying times, a piece of towelling and a piece of nylon material could be included.

Activity

The squares of cloth are wetted equally by having the same number of drops put on them. Ten drops are usually sufficient. The drops should be added carefully, waiting until each drop is absorbed by the cloth before the next drop is added. The drops should be evenly distributed over the area of the cloth. The pieces of cloth are then pinned or taped in the locations suggested.

When this has been done, the children are asked to predict which piece will dry first and why.

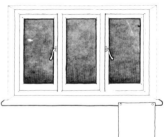

WATER

Activity 18   DRYING A WET CLOTH

You will need

a dropper
water
3 pieces of cloth each
15 cm square

● Put the same number of drops of water on each piece of cloth.

● Hang one piece of cloth in the classroom.
Hang one piece in a cold place in school.
Hang one piece outside.
In which place do you think the cloth will dry most quickly?
Why?
How long does each piece take to dry?

● Try this Activity again with different types of cloth. Hang them all in a good drying place and find out which type of cloth dries most quickly.

In your notebook write about what you did and what you found out.

page 23

After about half an hour the pieces of cloth are inspected to see whether they are dry.

Recording

Once the children have pinned out the pieces of cloth, they could describe in words and pictures what they have done and also what they expect to happen and why. The times taken for the pieces of cloth to dry in the different places are noted.

Follow-up

This Activity could be extended to investigate the drying times of other types of cloth. This could lead on to an investigation of cloth itself: the different sorts, the different ways it can be made, etc. The uses of different sorts of cloth could also provide interesting work. Clothes to keep us warm, to keep us cool, to keep us dry, and so on. Even the colour of clothes could be looked at.

ENERGY 1

Introduction

Energy is at the base of all science whether it be the study of living things, of ourselves, of chemical reactions, or of electricity. In all these different areas of science it is energy that we are really studying.

Energy is defined as the ability to do work. Nothing can be moved without the expenditure of energy. Energy can neither be created nor destroyed, but it can be converted from one form to another. Machines are devices for doing this. An electric vacuum cleaner, for example, is supplied with electrical energy. This is converted into mechanical energy which turns the fan or turbine. The fan causes a lowering of pressure, so air, dust and dirt are forced into the machine. The electrical energy supplied to the cleaner is first converted to mechanical energy and then into heat energy, mainly by friction. All energy is finally converted to heat energy.

The source of practically all our energy is the Sun. The other source of energy is from the breakdown of atoms in a nuclear reactor. The Sun's energy comes to us mainly in the form of light energy and heat energy. Light energy is used by plants in the manufacture of simple sugars and starches by a process called photosynthesis. The starches and sugars contain this energy from the Sun: it is locked up inside the molecules. When we eat and digest these molecules we release this energy for use by our bodies. Plants living on the Earth millions of years ago have now become the coal which we use as a fuel today. When the coal is burnt the energy is released again: this energy was 'trapped' by the plants millions of years ago.

In this first section on energy we introduce the children to the concept of energy in an oblique rather than a direct manner. The section begins with three drawings where balls are being used in different ways. In two of these drawings energy is being used to move the balls. The lady balancing the ball on her nose is not using energy to move the ball, but to keep it stationary.

In the first two Activities the children investigate bouncing balls: how many times different balls bounce and how the balls bounce on different surfaces.

Questions such as 'What do we have to do to keep a ball bouncing up and down?', 'What sort of ball bounces best?', 'What do we mean by "best", the ball which bounces the highest or the ball which bounces the greatest number of times?', will make the children think about what has to be done to start a ball bouncing and to keep it bouncing. In other words we can encourage them to think about energy.

These Activities provide some good scientific investigations and also introduce the very important point that the balls will only bounce when we have lifted them up (given them energy.) The balls will not move until we have given them energy. They cannot move by themselves.

In the next Activity the balls are allowed to roll down a slope. The angle of the slope is varied and the distance the balls travel is measured. It is then suggested that the board is laid flat and the ball placed at one end. The idea behind this is that it is only when the ball has been lifted up (given energy) that it will move.

The final part of the section on energy deals with model cars running down an incline. In the first Activity the children measure the distance the car travels with a gentle slope and then a steep slope. The final Activity is really a more refined version of the previous one. It shows the children how we can carry out a real scientific investigation.

These Activities are usually very successful with this age group. They quickly appreciate the need for repeating measurements at least three times and of finding ways of overcoming difficulties. The last class with which I did the

Activity with the cars moving down the slope carried the work over to the next day as they wanted to test their own model cars and lorries. They also found that if the slope was too steep the cars had a tendency to fall down the slope rather than run down it.

This section can be tackled by groups of four children to each set of apparatus. This could mean 9 or 10 groups and may cause difficulties with the available space. To overcome this difficulty the class can be split into two large groups and the work divided up among the children. It is possible to keep all the children actively involved in this way.

Activity 19   THE BEST BOUNCER

Aim

To involve the children in an Activity which takes a very familiar occurrence and investigates it in an objective manner.
To show the children the value of tabulation and measurement. To introduce the concept of energy.

Equipment

Instructions for making the simple metre stick are given in the construction notes.

Each group will require a lump of plasticine to support the metre stick, or the block stand suggested in the construction notes. Any sort of ball can be used. Those suggested in the Pupils' Books have been found to give interesting results.

Mastersheet

Each child will require a copy of Mastersheet 12.

Activity

Each group will require adequate space to carry out this Activity. I have used the school hall as this allows the groups to be well spaced out.

Before starting the Activity the children could be asked to predict which ball will be the best bouncer. The names of the different sorts of balls can be written on the blackboard and the number of children 'voting' for each ball can be added. At the end of the Activity a check could be made to see whose prediction was right.

A ball is held at the top of the metre stick and dropped (not thrown) on to the floor. The number of times the ball bounces is counted and this number is put on the Mastersheet. The same ball is dropped twice more and the number of bounces counted. The same procedure is followed with the other balls.

In the middle of page 25 the question 'What do you think will happen if you drop the balls from 2 metres high?' is asked. This investigation can be carried out under the direct supervision of the

teacher by one group while the other groups watch. Questions such as 'Do you think the ball will bounce twice as many times?' and 'How high do you think the ball will bounce?' can be asked before the balls are dropped.

Recording

A simple written description and a drawing could accompany the Mastersheet.

Follow-up

Would the number of bounces be more or less if we had thrown the ball? More, we would have given the ball more energy.

What do we have to do to any of the balls before they will bounce? We have to lift them up to the top of the metre stick. In other words we have to do work on the balls to give them energy.

Activity 20   BOUNCING BALLS

Aim

To allow the children to consider the relationship between a bouncing ball and the surface on which it is bouncing.

To give the children practice in predicting a result.

Predicting is not the same as guessing. Through questions and discussion before starting the Activity, the children can consider what will happen when a ball is dropped on a hard surface (concrete or wood) and a soft surface (carpet or foam plastic).

Mastersheet

Each child will require a copy of Mastersheet 13.

Equipment

It is not necessary for all the groups to be provided with all the materials on which the balls are to be dropped. If there are ten groups, then three squares of each material will be sufficient.

Activity

Before starting the Activity the children are asked to write down what they predict will happen. The procedure is then similar to that for Activity 19. If time allows, the balls can be dropped on to the different surfaces two or three times and a rough average taken. (Most seven year olds will not have tackled averages as such in their maths lessons, but they do know that if a ball bounces, say, 8, 8 and 7 times, then 8 is 'about right'.)

Note

When a ball hits a hard surface it loses little energy and bounces up again. If the surface is soft, the ball sinks into the surface, losing some of its energy as it pushes down. The ball now has less energy so will bounce less.

At the end of Activity 20 the two questions are to emphasise the fact that the balls will only

How many times does each ball bounce on the carpet, the wood, the foam, and the cotton wool?

13 Use Mastersheet 13 to record your results. Like this:

Ball	Number of bounces on:			
	carpet	wood	foam	cotton wool
tennis	2		1	
table tennis	3			

In your notebook write about what you did and what you found out about bouncing balls. Use the heading 'What did happen'.

Was it what you thought would happen?

How did you start the balls bouncing? Could the balls start bouncing by themselves?

bounce after we have given them energy by lifting them up and releasing them. The main point of Activities 19 and 20 is to show that movement results from an object being given energy. In the Activities we give energy to the balls by lifting them up.

Recording

A short description of what the children did, could accompany Mastersheet 13. The children should also look at their results on Mastersheet 13 and write down what they have found out.

Activity 21   ROLLING BALLS

Aim

To let the children measure the distances travelled by balls running down a slope and see that there is a relationship between the height of the slope and the distance the ball travels.
To demonstrate to the children that, unless we give the balls energy, they will not move and that the more energy we give them the greater the distance they will travel.

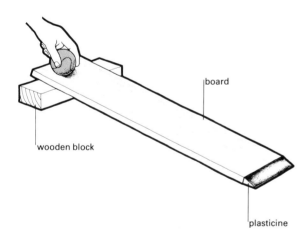

wooden block

board

plasticine

Equipment

The board is 1 metre long and 15cm wide.
The construction of a slope support is described in the construction notes. This can also be obtained from Supplier 1. Books or wooden blocks can also be used to support the ramp.

Where the edge of the board meets the floor, plasticine should be used to avoid a sudden drop. See the drawing on page 28 of the Pupils' Book.

Mastersheet

Each child will require a copy of Mastersheet 14.

Special note

Plenty of room is needed for this Activity. The school hall could be used. The smaller the size of the groups doing this Activity the better. Three or four children per group would be ideal. However, it can be done as a demonstration Activity with members of the class carrying out various jobs such as releasing the ball, measuring the distance travelled and so on.

Activity

Once the equipment has been set up, the children could be asked to predict what is going to happen. Bring to their attention the fact that, when the board is flat, the ball does not move.
The first slope should be quite gentle. Release one of the balls from the top and measure the distance it travels (from the top of the slope to where it comes to rest) to the nearest centimetre. To check this distance the ball should be rolled down the slope twice more. The children should record the results on Mastersheet 14.
The procedure should be repeated with the other balls.

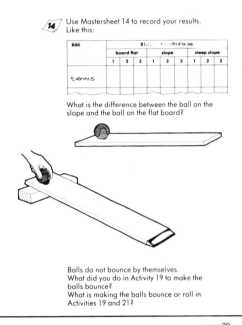

14 Use Mastersheet 14 to record your results.
Like this:

ball	Distance travelled in cm								
	board flat			slope			steep slope		
	1	2	3	1	2	3	1	2	3
tennis									

What is the difference between the ball on the slope and the ball on the flat board?

Balls do not bounce by themselves.
What did you do in Activity 19 to make the balls bounce?
What is making the balls bounce or roll in Activities 19 and 21?

page 29

The questions on page 29 should be considered once the Activity is completed.

Recording

A simple drawing could accompany the Mastersheet to give a record of what they did and what happened.

The important questions on page 29 could be copied by the children and after each question they could put in their own answer.

Activity 22   MODEL CARS

Activities 22 and 23 are arranged like this so that the children can see how we can get a general or qualitative result from an Activity and then, by refining our method, get a quantitative result.

Activity 22 can be carried out quite quickly and the general conclusion (which most children will be able to predict) that the steeper the slope the further the car will travel can be drawn.

It should be noted that it is not the steepness itself which is important. The steeper the slope, the higher the car has been lifted, and the more energy has been used to get the car to the top of the slope. The car therefore has more energy and travels further.

Aim
The main aim of the Activity is to get the children to predict what is going to happen and then to check whether their predictions are correct.

Another aim of this Activity is to point out to the children that it is important to check that something which seems quite obvious is true.

It is, perhaps, rather early to describe to the children Galileo's work on falling bodies, but one of his experiments could be described to show how sometimes what we think is going to happen does not.

Galileo wanted to find out if a heavy object falls faster than a lighter object. Many people would think that (everything else being equal) a heavy object would fall faster – it seems logical that this should happen. To check on this, Galileo took two cannon balls to the top of the Leaning Tower of Pisa. One ball was very much heavier than the other. He arranged for the balls to be dropped at exactly the same time and their landing at the bottom of the tower to be recorded. He found that, after repeating the experiment many times, both balls landed at the same time. Many people who saw this experiment or who read about it, still would not believe that a heavy object and a lighter object fall at the same rate. (This is only true if the air resistance is approximately the same for the two objects.)

Equipment

The model car can be purchased for about 50p in toyshops or can be borrowed from a member of the class. It is useful to have three or four cars as a part of the science resources of the school.

Activity

This Activity is best done as a demonstration. When the slope has been set up, the children can be asked how far they think the car will travel. This will be a guess rather than a prediction. The car is then released. The slope is made much steeper, predictions made and then checked.

Recording

From their predictions and tests the children should be encouraged to write a general conclusion. Some children will find this difficult to do and some help and discussion may be needed.

Activity 23   HOW HIGH AND HOW FAR?

I have found that this Activity generates a great deal of interest and excitement in the children and they like to extend the Activity by comparing various model cars and lorries. If you do allow this, make sure you have a good supply of Mastersheet 15.

Aim

To show how a simple Activity can be refined and carried out in a more 'scientific' manner. To summarise what has been learnt from the previous Activities in this section on energy. To give the class practical experience of measurement.

Mastersheet

Each child will require a copy of Mastersheet 15.

Activity

It is a good idea to start off with the board flat, in other words with no slope at all. Then the question 'Why doesn't the car move now?' could be asked.

The slope should then be adjusted to about 5cm high. The children could discuss where the height of the slope should be measured. The decision made here must, of course, apply to all the later measurements of the height of the slope. If using the ramp support described in the construction notes, the slope can be increased by one rung at a time.

Note that when the slope is quite steep the model cars will not run down the board. They slide or fall. This could be noted by the children. They must realise that these results cannot be used in conjunction with the measurements taken when the car was running down the slope.

Each measurement of the distance travelled is made three times. It will be found that they are fairly consistent providing everything else is kept constant.

To give some idea of the distances involved here are some results obtained by a class of seven-year-olds quite recently:

Height of top of slope (in cm)	Distance car travelled (in cm)		
	1	2	3
Red car			
7	128	127	127
22	257	257	257
42	279	269	279
White car			
7	116	119	117
22	208	196	227
42	289	286	287

The cars were running on to the carpeted floor of the classroom.

At the end of the Activity general conclusions can be drawn.

Recording

A drawing could accompany the Mastersheet. A short written description could also be made. If the class can make simple graphs, the results can be plotted on the centimetre graph paper from Mastersheet G/4. The distances travelled should be plotted on the vertical axis and the slope on the horizontal axis. A block graph or a simple line graph could be made. These graphs show very well the effect of increasing the slope on the distance travelled.

Introduction

It is possible to carry out a large number of activities concerned with the working of the human body. However, in a scheme of this sort it is necessary to be selective and to include only those activities which are both interesting to the children and provide good examples of scientific work.

In this section on 'ourselves' in year 1 we are going to look at the senses. The children will find out how we gather information about our immediate surroundings and how we use this information. We rarely use one sense in isolation. When we are eating a meal it is not only the taste of the foods but also their texture and smell which allow us to distinguish betwear them. The visual appearance of foods is also important. With some foods even the sound made by the food can be appetising. In this section, however, we are trying to isolate the senses and investigate, as far as possible, each of the five senses in turn.

One important word of warning: in this section due care and attention must be given to hygiene. This applies particularly to the Activity on tasting.

The section opens with a double page spread of drawings of various sorts of animals. These drawings can be used to make children realise that we, as human beings, are a part of the natural world. We are animals and in many ways we behave in the same way as other animals. A useful discussion could be held with the children about the ways (good and bad) in which we differ from the other animals. (In the 'Animals' sections of the Pupils' Books the children will be looking at some animals and their senses.) From these pictures and the discussion a list of the senses can be made up. The children cut out the pictures which are repeated on Mastersheets 16 and 17, mount them in their books and write underneath the senses the animals have.

The following Activities are best carried out as a 'circus' as described earlier in this book (page 9).

Activity 24   WHAT IS IT?

Many children will have already used a 'feelie box' of some sort. However, here we are going to use it in a particular way, probably a different way from that met in the infant school.

Aim

To concentrate the children's attention on their sense of touch and to discover that, although we can get a great deal of information about a material from just feeling it, there are limits to what the sense of touch alone can tell us.

Equipment

The feelie box is described in the construction notes or can be purchased from Supplier 1. The main point about the box is that the child using it cannot see what he or she is feeling or touching but the window allows his or her partner to check the materials being used.

The envelopes could contain:

Envelope 1
Pieces of paper with distinct and different textures –

1 smooth, glossy paper
2 rough, brown paper
3 newspaper or a paper towel
4 sandpaper
5 writing paper

Envelope 2
Pieces of paper and card of similar texture but of different thicknesses –

1 tissue paper
2 writing paper
3 thin card (exercise book cover)
4 thick card
5 strawboard

Envelope 3
Different types of material –
1 a piece of velvet cloth
2 a piece of knitted material
3 a piece of expanded polystyrene (ceiling tile)
4 a piece of polythene sheeting
5 a piece of linen (or similar).

Mastersheet

Each child will require a copy of Mastersheet 18.

Activity

The children should work in pairs. The first child puts his or her hands into the feelie box with Envelope 1. The window of the feelie box should be facing the partner. On opening the envelope, the child takes each material in turn and describes what it feels like. The partner puts these words down on Mastersheet 18 as described in the pupils' text. When all the pieces have been used they are returned to the envelope. The partners now change places and use Envelope 2 in the same way. Alternating in this way, each child uses all three envelopes. The fact that the children will have seen the contents of some of the envelopes before using them in the feelie box does not seem to spoil this Activity. Of course, other envelopes could be prepared so that each child uses fresh materials, but I have not found this to be necessary.

The sort of things the sense of touch cannot tell us are the colour of the materials and whether they have a smell.

Recording

A drawing of the feelie box could accompany the results which the partners write down. There could also be a short statement about the limitations of the sense of touch.

Activity 25   WHAT IS THE SMELL?

Aim

To show the children that we can identify many substances by smell but that we are unable to detect any smell from some other substances.

Equipment

Two sets of five jars per group.

In Set 1 the five jars are labelled 1-5 and should contain substances with easily identifiable smells. Examples are instant coffee, vinegar, onion, orange, peppermint (essence).

The second set should contain two substances which we can identify by smell and three substances which we cannot identify by smell. Examples are salt, sugar, flour, tomato, potato.

These are labelled A-E. Included in this set could be something such as a piece of soap which has a perfume, but the perfume does not allow us to identify it. Talcum powder could also be used.

So that items such as instant coffee and sugar cannot be identified visually, each jar could contain a pad of cotton wool with the substance in the middle. Do not forget to keep a record of what is in each jar. The best type of jar for this work is that in which some varieties of baby food are sold.

Cover the open top of each jar with a piece of linen or bandage held in place with an elastic band.

Mastersheet

Each child will require a copy of Mastersheets 19 and 20.

Activity

The children smell each of the jars in turn, Set 1 first. They write what they think is in each jar in the Mastersheet table. Later they can check this with you.

Then they use jars A-E. The idea of this set of jars is to get the children to realise that some substances cannot be identified by smell. Quite often these substances can be identified by taste (salt).

Recording

The children could write a short description of what they did and what they found out. This could accompany Mastersheets 19 and 20.

Activity 26   WHAT DOES IT TASTE OF?

Aim

To let the children investigate the sense of taste and to introduce the idea that the tongue can only detect four tastes: sweet, sour, bitter and salt.

Equipment

Hygiene is most important here and this should be carefully explained to the children.

Any common foods are suitable. If we keep to the foods which are white and in powder form there is no need for a blindfold to prevent visual identification of the food. Examples are icing sugar, flour, salt, 'Instant Whip' (various flavours), 'instant' potato.

The foods can be placed in small piles on tin lids or on squares of paper. They should be numbered 1-5. The child places small amounts of each food on his or her tongue. As the food is identified it is recorded on Mastersheet 21.

Mastersheet

Each child will require a copy of Mastersheet 21.

Follow-up

As well as being able to taste food we can also sense texture. Through a combination of taste, texture, smell and visual appearance we are able to get a total impression of the food. It is our reaction to this total impression that determines whether we like the food or not.

Activity 27   BE A SOUND DETECTIVE!

Aim

To get children to identify objects by the sounds they make without actually seeing them. Also to get the children to deduce the shape and texture of objects by the way the objects move in a closed box.

Equipment

The net shown in the construction notes can be used to make up the Mystery Boxes. Four to six boxes are needed. Each net should be drawn out on fairly thick card and the fold lines scored. The net should be cut out and all the tabs glued into position except one. Finally, after putting in the objects, the lid should be glued down. One empty, open box will be needed in each set for the children to test their inferences.

The boxes can be arranged in sets in which some contain objects which are more difficult to identify. To help the children, a duplicate set of the objects in the boxes should be provided. To make the identification a little more difficult, a few extra objects could be included with these loose objects.

Suitable objects for a relatively easy set of boxes are:

Box 1 – Empty
Box 2 – 1 ball bearing or marble
Box 3 – 2 ball bearings or marbles
Box 4 – 1 piece of cardboard
Box 5 – 2 pieces of cardboard
Box 6 – 2 ball bearings or marbles and 2 pieces of cardboard

Mastersheet

Each child will require a copy of Mastersheet 22.

Activity

The children are supplied with a set of boxes and a tray on which is a duplicate set of the objects in the boxes. By listening to the sounds made by the objects as the boxes are moved, the children try to identify them. To check their identification they put the objects in the empty box to see whether they make the same noises. Mastersheet 22 is used to record what they think is in the boxes. When they have finished they check with the teacher to find out if they were right or wrong. (Remember to keep a record of the contents of the boxes.)

I have found this Activity to be very popular with the children and, simple though it is, it does give them excellent practice in observing, making inferences and then testing the correctness of their inferences.

Activity 28   SEEING

Aim

To show the children that we can only distinguish objects of a certain size within a certain range.

Equipment

Each group needs a set of cards. Each card should have a dot in the middle marked with black felt-tip pen. The cards should be of white cardboard. The dots could be the following sizes: 2mm, 5mm, 10mm and 20mm. One card can be left blank. The blank card can be used to check whether the person being tested is identifying correctly. This is not a test of honesty as such. If we know we are trying to see a dot on a card from a distance, our imagination can come into action and we may 'see' a dot which is not actually present.

If the children are to make a graph of their findings, they will need Mastersheet G/4 (the centimetre-squared paper). The children can use metre tapes made up from Mastersheet G/5 or the longer tapes often available in schools.

Mastersheet

Each child will require a copy of Mastersheet 23.

Activity

The cards should be jumbled up so that the dots do not appear in order of size. If time allows each distance measurement should be repeated three times.

Follow-up

Does colour matter? What would happen if we used white dots on a black background, or red dots on a yellow background?

Introduction

The environment in which we live can be divided into the natural environment and that part which has been created by humans. In urban areas the man-made structures dominate, while in rural areas it is the natural world which is more obvious.

This section is an introduction to the materials which are available to build structures and also to the way in which humans have learned to use these materials to build structures which are strong and carry out the functions for which they were designed.

In this book the pupils investigate some of the structural properties of a material which most of them think of as being inherently weak – paper. When carrying out these Activities with children one aspect always seems to appear: their suprise that paper can be made to support relatively heavy weights quite easily. In the final Activity a stool which is strong enough to support any child in the class and even the teacher is built from newspaper! This Activity is certainly a 'fun' Activity, but it does have a 'serious' message: that paper, when used and shaped in particular ways, can support heavy weights.

The most suitable type of paper for these Activities is A4 duplicating paper. A 500 sheet pack will usually be sufficient for a class working in groups of three or four. The weights (masses) used in these Activities can be marbles, ball bearings or manufactured 'weights'. The problem with using manufactured weights is that a very large number will be needed for all the groups. A good alternative is to use marbles. Contact a local toy wholesaler to find out if they will sell you marbles in large quantities (1000 – 1500 at least). Storage of the marbles is a problem and the best solution I have come up with is to buy a number of cheap plastic boxes with lids, such as those designed for keeping food in the freezer. Each box can contain 100 or 200 marbles. They can be easily distributed to the groups and just as easily collected again. I have numbered the boxes I use so that I can occasionally check up the marbles are not 'disappearing'. Marbles vary in their weight according to the manufacturer: most of them of the size normally encountered are about 5g in weight. In the practical work in this section we say the weight is 5g even though this is not quite accurate. A high degree of accuracy is not important in this work. It is the relative weights which are important not the actual weights.

Paper tubes can be very strong and some of the tubes the children make in these Activities can support as much as 1.5kg – about 330 marbles!

The Activities described in this section are generally enjoyed by children of this age group. They also provide us with some excellent opportunities for discussing with the children ways of carrying out 'fair testing' and collecting information and results. Further, they give the children the opportunity to look at numbers and get information from these numbers. The children will see numbers 'in action'.

One point must be emphasised. The numbers we use here are not just numbers, they are numbers of things. Even at this early age we should insist that the children always write down

STRUCTURES

When you use your science book you are using one of the world's greatest inventions – paper.

Paper has been made for hundreds of years. It has been used to write on, paint on, and print on. Paper is very useful but we do not think of it as being strong.

Do you think paper is strong?

How many people in your class think paper is strong?
How many think paper is weak?
Write down the answer.

By the time we have finished this section perhaps some people will have changed their minds!

page 41

the units of measurement, whether it be 200 marbles, 200 sheets of paper or 200 grams.

Page 41 of the Pupils' Book is an introduction to the section. It is intended to get the children to think about a property of paper that they have not considered before its strength. They have used paper in many different ways but probably never as a strong supporting material.

Leading from this introductory work, I have found it interesting to discuss with the children how many different sorts of paper we use in the classroom, in the school as a whole and at home. We have made collections of different sorts of paper and both the class and I have been surprised to find just how many different sorts there are. The collection can provide valuable opportunities for display, classification, labelling and so on. Writing to paper manufacturers can often result in useful display material for the classroom.

Activity 29   FOLDING PAPER

Aim

To show the children that, by merely making one fold in a sheet of paper, we can change its properties.

Equipment

Each child will need two or three sheets of paper, a piece of card about 20cm square and a yoghurt pot or something similar.

Activity

It is interesting to see the difference between folding the paper lengthwise and widthwise. When the paper is folded across its width the base is small compared with the height and it can only support a small weight. If the paper is folded across its length it is much stronger and can support more weight.

Activity 30   MAKING PAPER STRONG

Aim

To let the children investigate the effect of making two folds in the paper.
To impress on the children the importance of testing the paper structure 'fairly'. (Each structure is tested in exactly the same way, using the same piece of card and the same pot. Only the number of marbles is varied.)

Equipment

The pieces of card needed for the Activity should be quite firm but not thick and heavy. Each group will need a maximum of one hundred marbles, though the number will, of course, depend on the weight of the individual marbles. Other weights could be used such as notebooks or, if they are available in sufficient numbers, 5g weights.

One word of warning: it is important that the children collect up marbles which fall on the floor as soon as they fall. Marbles on the classroom floor can be dangerous to people moving around. The children could use books to make a 'wall' round their testing area to prevent marbles rolling off the table.

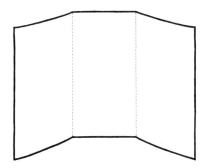

Activity

A sheet of A4 paper is folded twice across the width. The edges are held together with small pieces of sticky tape (about 2cm long). It is important to emphasise the size of the sticky tape used: if the pieces of tape are too big we might be testing the strength of the paper plus the sticky tape. If the pieces of tape are very small in comparison with the sheet of paper we can reasonably ignore them as strengtheners.

Recording

A simple description with some drawings of what they did could be followed by a statement of what they have found out.

If you decide to extend the Activity (as suggested on page 44 of the Pupils' Book) by using different sorts of paper, this should also be recorded. Remember to keep the testing fair. All other factors apart from the type of paper should be kept constant.

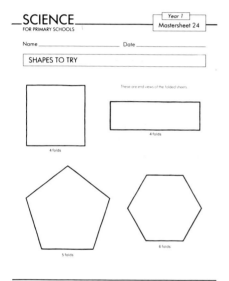

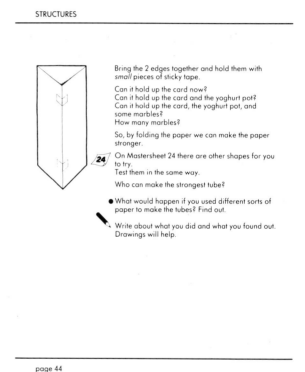

page 44

After the children have tested the triangular shape, they can go on to try some of the shapes shown on Mastersheet 24. Each group could, perhaps, try two other shapes.

Activity 31   HOW STRONG ARE PAPER TUBES?

Aim

To let the children discover that, even without folding the sheet of paper, changing the shape can make a stronger structure.
To introduce the idea of variables: in this case the variable is the diameter of the tube.

Activity

The children will probably be very surprised at the weight the larger tubes will support. This can be as much as 1.5kg. You may find it necessary to replace some of the marbles with 500g weights. If these weights are of the flat

metal variety, the pot of marbles can stand on top.

The narrow tube should not be too narrow, otherwise, with the card and pot on top, it will tip over.

If marbles are used as weights, the children should be reminded to guard the experimental area with, say, books, in order to prevent their being scattered.

Recording

A drawing showing how the tubes were tested can be followed by a simple written record of the weights the tubes supported before they collapsed.

Activity 32   TESTING PAPER TUBES

Aim

The previous Activities in this section have been concerned with testing paper structures in a rather general way. In this Activity the aim is to let the children use a more refined method of testing. The formers (wooden rods) are used so that one variable (the diameter of the tube) is kept constant. This is an important part of the scientific method which can be brought to the children's attention here.

Another aim of this Activity is to get the children to think of the various ways in which we can test a material or structure. In this simple example the tube can be tested in two ways: across the width and across the length.

Equipment

The wooden formers are 30cm lengths of 12-15mm and 25mm dowel rod.

The paper tubes can be supported on piles of books or wooden blocks. The construction of support stands is described in the construction notes.

The pots to hold the marbles are best prepared beforehand as they are too difficult for children of this age to make. Plastic drinking cups or yoghurt pots are suitable. First make four evenly spaced holes around the top of the pot with the point of a steel knitting needle which has been heated. Thread a length of string through each hole. Make a knot at one end of each piece of string to prevent it slipping through the hole.

Now knot all four strings together over the pot. Try to get all the strings knotted at an equal distance from the pot. Cut off the extra string from three pieces, but leave the fourth piece long enough to tie in a loop which will fit over the paper tube.

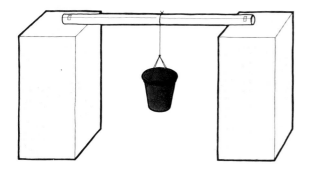

Activity

The drawing on page 47 of the Pupils' Book shows the set-up, but it is better to show this to the children with the actual equipment they will use. Show them how to make the paper tubes and emphasise the use of *small* pieces of sticky tape. Also discuss with the children the importance of keeping the support stands the same distance apart while testing the tubes. As the paper is twenty-one centimetres wide (if you are using A4 paper) the support stands can be fifteen centimetres apart. This allows three centimetres of tube to rest on each stand.

The marbles should be placed, not dropped, into the pot. The tubes do not break but collapse in the middle. Each width of tube should be tested three times.

Remember to arrange some way of catching the marbles when the tubes collapse.

Recording

A drawing similar to that on page 47 of the Pupils' Book will be sufficient to remind the children of what they did. The results could be written under the drawing along with a written statement about what they found out.

Follow-up

If time allows, the children could test other tubes in the same way:
1 using different-sized formers to make tubes of different widths
2 using different sorts of paper: newspaper, wrapping paper, tissue paper.

Activity 33 MAKING A PAPER STOOL

Aim

This is a fun Activity with a serious aim: to show the children how they can use their knowledge of how to increase the strength of paper (by forming it into tubes) to make a structure strong enough to support their own weight.

Equipment

As each child will want to make his or her own stool, plenty of newspaper will be needed. The twenty-two sheets for each stool must be from the same newspaper. The other important requirements are a supply of sticky tape and plenty of room. If you can use the school hall for this Activity then so much the better.

Activity

The children need to work in pairs.

When testing the stools it is important that they are vertical and the child testing the stool should hold on to a table or their partner until they are sure their stool is safe. These stools will support an average adult so they are quite strong enough to support a young child.

The reason for the children weighing themselves is to bring a quantitative aspect to this Activity.

ACTIVITIES

Book 1B

AIR

Introduction

In this section on the air we are mainly concerned with clarifying in the children's minds the idea that the air is something more than just empty space. Most of the Activities are based on occurrences which are already familiar to the children but which are now looked at more thoughtfully.

Some work on the air is generally included in the science course of any school. This work can include the following topics.

1 Air and water are the two essentials for the basic life processes of animals and plants.
2 Combining the work from the Water section with the work from this section, the children can get some understanding of the weather and how this affects our lives.
3 Air can also be useful as a source of energy. Moving air can turn the sails of a windmill and this movement can be harnessed to turn other machinery and do work.
4 If we have an understanding of air pressure and the effects of differences in air pressure, we can begin to have some idea of how aeroplanes, insects, birds and bats fly.
5 An understanding of the effect of heat on air explains why hot-air balloons rise in the air and why convection currents are set up.

Activity 34   MAKING A PAPER WINDMILL

Aim

To provide practice for the children in following instructions, cutting with scissors and manipulating wire.

Equipment

The cheapest source of sticks is a garden centre. The thin sticks used for supporting pot plants are very suitable.

The beads must have a hole through which the wire from a paper clip will pass easily.

Mastersheet

A copy of Mastersheet 25 will be required by each pupil as the main part of the windmill is cut from the Mastersheet. The instructions are also printed on the Mastersheet.

SCIENCE
FOR PRIMARY SCHOOLS

Year 1
Mastersheet 25

Name _____ Date _____

MAKING A PAPER WINDMILL

1 Cut out a piece of paper 15 cm square.
2 Join the corners with pencil lines.
3 Make holes at A, B, C, D and E.
4 Cut along the pencil lines from the corners towards the middle. Stop cutting about 3 cm from the middle.
5 Straighten out the wire paper clip.
6 Twist it round the top of the stick.
7 Thread a bead on to the wire.
8 Put the wire through hole E, then bend over the corners in turn and thread A, B, C and D on to the wire.
9 Thread on the other bead and bend the wire over.

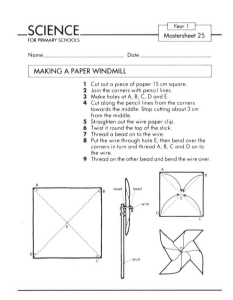

Activity

The holes in the square cut from the Mastersheet are best made with a punch: a leather punch adjusted to make a fairly small hole is easiest to use. Before the paper is actually bent over to make the windmill, the children may like to decorate it with crayons, coloured pencils or felt-tip pens. Do not let them use paint as this will crumple the paper and make it unsuitable for use. Although the children should each make a windmill they need to work in pairs.

The paper cilp should be opened out to make a straight piece of wire. One end should be bent over and a bead threaded on. The wire should be inserted through the four holes in the 'sails' and then through the central hole. A second bead should be put on the wire and the end of the wire bent round the stick. It may be necessary to hold the wire in place with some sticky tape.

The windmill can be tested by blowing on it, by holding it in the wind or by running with it. The sails are made to turn by moving air or by movement of the windmill through the air.

Recording

The children could write about how they made their windmill and how they made it turn. They could also add drawings.

Follow-up

Work could follow here on the way windmills were used to grind corn. Their use in Holland to pump water could also be mentioned.

Activity 35　BLOWING UP A BALLOON

Warning: this Activity can prove to be very noisy as most children know that air escaping from a balloon can produce weird noises if the neck is held in a particular way. You may well decide to carry out this Activity as a demonstration involving as many children as possible.

Aim

To get the children to think about a fairly common event in a rather different way. Usually when a balloon is being blown up, it is the party or other celebration that is uppermost in the children's minds. Here we are using the inflation of the balloon as evidence of the material nature of the air.

Equipment

Soft, pliable, easily inflated balloons are required. It is sometimes possible, particularly at Christmas time, to purchase balloons which are specially made for young children to inflate. Alternatively, a 'party balloon pump' might be used.

Warning: Do not allow children to use balloons which have previously been inflated by another child. There is an obvious risk of spreading colds etc. by this means.

AIR

Activity

The physical part of the Activity is quite straightforward. It is the consideration and discussion of the questions (and answers) on page 6 of the Pupils' Book which make the Activity relevant and important. Much of the work involved is used to stretch the rubber of the balloon, but we are also pumping air at pressure into the balloon against the pressure of the external air.

Prodding the balloon with a finger helps the children to get the 'feel' not only of the rubber pushing back, but of the inner air pushing back. Actually holding the balloon between the two hands gives a feeling of the material nature of the air.

Releasing the balloon is fun. The balloon shoots away in a direction opposite to that in which the air is released. This is a simple demonstration of the principle behind the jet engine.

Recording

Some simple drawings showing the balloon being blown up and also being released and flying away could be made. In addition, sentences giving answers to the questions on page 6 should be written after the class discussion.

Activity 35 BLOWING UP A BALLOON

You will need
a balloon

Your balloon will be floppy when you get it. Why?
Blow up your balloon.
What has happened?
Where has the air which is now in the balloon come from?

● When you have blown up your balloon, hold the neck tight.
Prod the balloon with your finger.
What is pushing on your finger from inside the balloon?

● Let the balloon go.
What did the balloon do?
What did the air do?

Write about what you did and what you found out. Use drawings.

page 6

Special note: The remaining Activities in this section could be combined and organised as a circus.

Activity 36   WHAT IS IN THE JAR?

Note

If the Activities are being organised as a circus, Activity 37 should be done straight after Activity 36, as these two Activities are very closely linked.

Aim

To provide the children with convincing evidence of the material nature of the air by trapping and then manipulating some air below water.

Mastersheet

Each child will require a copy of Mastersheet 26.

Equipment

The aquarium must contain sufficient water to cover the jar being used. Suitable jars are those sold in department stores and supermarkets for picnic drinks: they are usually quite strong and relatively inexpensive. They must, however, be of

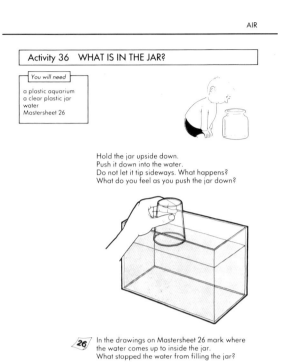

Activity 36   WHAT IS IN THE JAR?

You will need

a plastic aquarium
a clear plastic jar
water
Mastersheet 26

Hold the jar upside down.
Push it down into the water.
Do not let it tip sideways. What happens?
What do you feel as you push the jar down?

26 In the drawings on Mastersheet 26 mark where
the water comes up to inside the jar.
What stopped the water from filling the jar?

page 7

the clear variety. Glass jam jars are also suitable
but some teachers may be worried about
children of this age using glass containers.

Recording

Mastersheet 26 has four drawings showing the
container being lowered into the water. The
children complete the drawings by:

1 putting in the water levels
2 writing the word 'air' to show the air trapped
in the submerged container.

The children could write sentences to answer the
questions at the bottom of page 7 of the Pupils'
Book.

Activity 37   WHAT COMES OUT OF THE JAR?

Aim

To allow the children to manipulate a quantity of
air trapped below water.

Equipment

As for Activity 36 except that two jars are
required.

Mastersheet

Each child will require a copy of Mastersheet 27.

Activity

One jar is sunk, mouth upwards, in the
aquarium so that it fills with water. This is then
turned so that the mouth is downwards. The
second jar is submerged mouth first as in Activity
36. The pupil then holds a jar with each hand and

by gradually tipping the jars with their mouths
close together, transfers the air from one jar to
the other and back again.

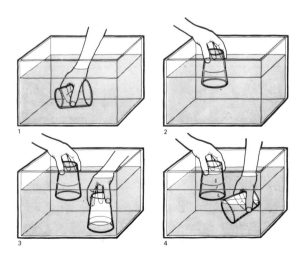

Recording

On Mastersheet 27 there are drawings of the jars. The children are told to colour the water blue and to leave the 'air' areas white. The children could also write about what they have done.

Activity 38   WHAT IS IN THE BOTTLE?

Aim

To provide the children with further evidence of the material nature of the air.

Equipment

The funnel should be of rigid plastic and either plasticine or Blu-tack can be used as a sealant. It is essential that the funnel is properly sealed into the neck of the bottle.

Activity

It is advisable for the teacher to check the equipment to see that a good seal has been made.

A jar of water is quickly poured into the funnel. Bubbles of air will come up through the water in the funnel and water will run into the bottle. Eventually, (if the seal is airtight) the air inside the bottle prevents further water from entering. If a small hole is made in the plasticine or Blu-tack seal with a piece of wire, air escapes and the water can enter.

If using the circus organisation as suggested on page 58, each group should be instructed to empty the water from the bottle and to reseal the funnel in the bottle before they move on to the next Activity.

Recording

The children could make a simple drawing to show the funnel sealed in the bottle and describe in words what they did and what they found out.

Activity 39   BLOWING INTO THE BOTTLE

Aim

To show the children that air can be compressed (but only by a small amount).

Activity

A fairly small glass bottle with a narrow neck is half filled with water. A plastic drinking straw is sealed in the neck with plasticine. The pupil blows down the straw as hard as he or she can. When the blowing stops, water is forced up through the straw. This is because the compressed air expands until it is at the same pressure as the air outside the bottle. In doing so it pushes the water up the straw. Remember that each child will need a fresh straw.

Recording

The children could make a drawing of the bottle, water and straw. Beneath the drawing they could write about what they did and what happened.

Activity 40   LOOKING AT AIR

Aim

To make the children think about the existence of air.

Equipment

The plastic washing-up liquid bottle should be well washed out and should have its jet intact. When purchasing plastic tubing for this Activity it is best to take the jet to the shop to make sure the plastic tubing is a really tight fit. To get a good seal between the jet and the tubing, warm the end of the tubing in some hot water for a minute or two. It will then become soft and flexible and will easily fit over the jet. As it cools and contracts it will grip the jet firmly.

Activity

This Activity 'works' because of alterations in the air pressure inside the plastic bottle. The children can be introduced to the Activity in terms of feeling and seeing air moving.

The children are asked at the beginning of the Activity if the bottle is empty. The answer is, of course, that it is empty of washing-up liquid, but full of air. As the child squeezes the bottle, air will bubble out through the water. More squeezing will cause more air to be expelled. When the bottle is released, water (forced by the external air pressure), rushes up the tube and into the bottle.

At the end of the Activity the bottle will contain water and air.

Recording

This could be a simple drawing followed by a few sentences describing what the children did, what happened and what they found out.

Air pictures (pages 12 and 13)

The pictures on these two pages are for class discussion: they are all connected in one way or another with air and the effects of air. At the end of the discussion a possible follow-up is for the class to draw and paint their own pictures on the theme 'Air' to produce a classroom display.

Windmill

This connects with Activity 34. The pressure of the moving air acting on the sails causes them to turn. In general terms, the stronger the wind, the faster the sails will turn. In this country windmills were used mainly to grind corn, but in Holland they are used to pump water and to prevent flooding of the very flat land. Modern windmills have been produced to convert the energy from the wind into electrical energy: they have had varying degrees of success.

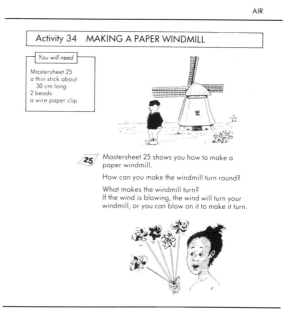

AIR

Activity 34   MAKING A PAPER WINDMILL

You will need

Mastersheet 25
a thin stick about
    30 cm long
2 beads
a wire paper clip

25 Mastersheet 25 shows you how to make a paper windmill.

How can you make the windmill turn round?

What makes the windmill turn?
If the wind is blowing, the wind will turn your windmill, or you can blow on it to make it turn.

page 5

Racing yacht

The large sails on yachts are designed to 'catch' the wind so that the force of the wind can be used to drive the yacht through the water.

Parachute

The 'umbrella' of the parachute provides a large air-resistant surface which reduces the parachutist's rate of descent. Parachutes have holes or slots in them so that air can escape slowly and allow a smooth descent. Without these holes the parachutist would be swung about as the air escaped from under the umbrella. By manipulating the strings of the parachute and the slots an experienced parachutist is able to steer the parachute and land in a predetermined place.

Storm damage

When air is moving at very high speeds it can cause terrible damage to buildings and trees. This picture provides very vivid evidence of the physical nature of the air: air is certainly not just empty space.

Kite

A kite is light in weight. It flies because differences in movement of the air above and below the kite produce differences in pressure, so giving it 'lift'. The size of a kite can vary from a few centimetres to many metres. There are a number of books available which give instructions for making simple kites. The children could try making some of these and in flying them would not only get considerable enjoyment, but would also feel the air acting on the kite.

Glider

A glider has to be launched into the air. Once in the air, lift is maintained by use of warm air currents (thermals) and the movement of the air over the wing surfaces. The wings of gliders are longer than those of powered planes: the lift in a powered aircraft is produced mainly by the air being forced over the shaped wing surfaces.

Diver

If we leave our air-filled environment and enter the sea, we must take our own supply of air.

Astronaut

When an astronaut ventures outside the spacecraft (which has to carry a supply of air) he or she must take a supply of air in a backpack as there is no air in space. An astronaut also has to be protected against the reduced air pressure in space. Without a spacesuit an astronaut would explode, as the human body is adapted to exist in the normal air pressure of Earth.

Misty day

This picture ties up with Activity 16 in the Water section of Book 1A. Under certain conditions of temperature and humidity, the water in the air condenses into minute drops and it is these which constitute mist. If the mist also contains pollutants such as smoke and car exhaust fumes then smog or fog result.

WATER

| Activity 16   WHERE DOES THE WATER GO? |

Your teacher will show you this Activity. Watch carefully and think about what is happening.

● First, your teacher will put some ice in a jar. What will the ice do to the jar?

● Your teacher will then stand the jar in a dish.

● What do you see on the outside of the jar? What do you think this is? Where has it come from?

Now, when the washing dries,
when the puddle dries up,
when water 'disappears' from a bottle,
where does the water go?

page 20

Introduction

Children are naturally interested in living things, particularly animals. In the classroom we can utilise this interest to get children involved in some good scientific activities.

However, our aims in carrying out this work on animals with our classes should not be confined to purely scientific ones. For example, it is important that the children develop a respect for other living things and realise that these living things have their own part to play in the web of life. The destruction of animals and plants can seriously affect the balance of life. The various forms of life are dependent on each other. If one animal or plant ceases to exist the effect may be very far-reaching. As a simple example, the massive use of insecticides by farmers in recent years has seriously affected the bee population. This in turn has meant that the flowers of fruit-bearing trees are not fertilised, resulting in poor fruit crops.

Many children and adults have strong fears or dislikes of certain animals. Snakes and spiders are high on the list of the most feared animals. These fears have some justification: some spiders, though certainly not in this country, have a poisonous bite which can have unpleasant if not fatal results. Snakes can kill either with their venom or by crushing. Nevertheless, these creatures are essential parts of the complicated jigsaw of life. Human beings, the most highly developed members of the animal kingdom, have the power to destroy any other form of life (with certain exceptions) and have a heavy responsibility to these other members. It is this responsible approach which we should try to foster in our pupils. It is a matter of having respect for all other living things: they have a right to live as much as we have. Sometimes, of course, human beings do kill other animals. It may be that we need the meat for food: many children are very shocked when they first realise that the meat they are eating has come from a once living animal which had to be killed. Some children are so shocked that they refuse to eat meat and become vegetarian at least for a while.

Other animals have to kill to live. All carnivorous animals, such as lions and tigers, kill other animals for food.

We have to kill some animals which can damage our health. Parasites such as fleas and lice are prime examples. Rats and mice which may invade our homes and spoil our food supplies are another case for justified killing. Houseflies, tse-tse flies and mosquitoes are all animals which we kill to prevent the spread of disease.

We must encourage our pupils to respect all living things, killing only when absolutely necessary, and then in the most humane manner possible, and never being cruel to any animal however lowly it may be.

The Activities in this section are concerned with two animals which are quite easily found all over the country: earthworms and snails. They are also two animals which suffer from maltreatment by both adults and children. It is our duty as teachers to ensure that, if we use these creatures in the classroom, we make absolutely sure that they do not suffer in any way while in our care. The children's attitude will certainly reflect their family's treatment of animals of this sort, but at this age the children are probably strongly influenced by their teacher. A caring, humane attitude displayed by a teacher will have an immediate effect on most children. Teachers have a heavy responsibility towards the children in their classes and towards the animals brought into the classroom for study purposes.

The snails and worms should both be carefully housed and fed, and when they have been studied, returned to the places where they were found.

There is always the problem of the child or children who do not like snails and worms. Usually, at this stage, this is easily overcome – not by forcing the children to pick up the animals, but by showing them that they have nothing to fear from these creatures. (If the teacher does not like the animals it is probably better to omit this section: it is no good acting an attitude to children. If you do not like worms and snails then the children will quickly realise this.) If your example does not alter the children's attitude then I have found it is best to leave these children to overcome their fears or dislikes in their own good time. They will watch other children handling the animals and gradually build up their own courage until they finally pick up a snail or a worm and discover that it is not nasty or unpleasant.

The Activities in this section are concerned with the animals' behaviour. They may be relatively simple animals, but they nevertheless have sense organs to find out about their immediate environment. This work can be related to the section on 'Ourselves' in Book 1A, where we are looking at our senses.

The work in this section needs some forward planning. For example, before the children go out of the classroom to collect the animals, you must make sure that all the materials for making homes for these animals are available. Food must also be available. The homes for the animals must provide conditions as close to those in their natural environment as possible. With both snails and earthworms one essential condition is that they are kept damp. When the children are handling the earthworms (which they should do as infrequently as possible) their hands should be damp.

Activity 41 FINDING EARTHWORMS

Aim

To collect earthworms for further study in the classroom.
To see the conditions under which earthworms normally live so that they can be housed in similar conditions in the classroom.

Note

It may not be possible in some schools for the teacher to take the class out and actually find the worms in their natural habitat. In this case, arrangements could be made with the Parks Department of the local council or with a parent who has a garden or allotment to provide some earthworms.

Equipment

For this initial Activity it is suggested that the group size could be quite large. Groups of about eight children could each set up a wormery. Thus, with a class of thirty-two children, four wormeries would be needed, or five with a class of forty.

Each group should have a plastic box with a clip-on lid. The sort used for keeping food in the freezer or refrigerator is very suitable. Each box should be about half full of damp soil.

Forks are suggested for digging up the worms as there is less likelihood of cutting the worms than if trowels were used. Hand forks are quite suitable unless the ground is very hard.

If the weather has been particularly dry the worms may have burrowed deeply into the soil and may therefore be rather difficult to dig up. In this case the ground should be moistened with water. The worms will come up to the surface to avoid waterlogged ground. Allow at least ten to fifteen minutes after watering before digging up the worms.

Activity

The children need to be told that they should not pull the worms out of the ground. It is better to gently push them on to a sheet of paper. At all times we should emphasise the need for care in handling the animals.

Recording

In their notebooks the children could describe where they found the worms, how they found them and how they brought them back into the classroom.

Activity 42   A HOME FOR WORMS

Aim

To emphasise to the children the importance of carefully planning homes for animals which we wish to study: that these homes should be as close as possible to the conditions under which the animals live in their natural state.
To foster in the children a caring attitude towards all living things.

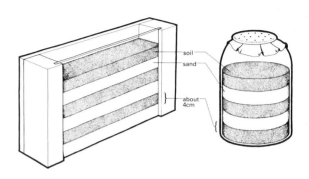

Equipment

Wormeries in which we can keep the animals for a *short* period of time can be:
1 made from large plastic sweet jars
2 made from wood and clear plastic (see construction notes at the end of this book)
3 purchased from suppliers.

Plastic sweet jars

These should first be washed out and dried.

Layers of sandy soil and dark loam are put into the jar. The layers should be pressed down but not too hard. If difficulty is experienced in obtaining a light-coloured sandy soil (to provide a clear visual contrast with the dark loam) then sand can be obtained from a garden centre. This should be washed to remove any soluble impurities before it is put into the wormery. Each layer should be about 4cm deep and the jar should be about two-thirds full. The soil must be quite damp and should never be allowed to dry out while the worms are living in it.

A cover can be made from black sugar paper. This can be in the form of a tube which can be placed over the jar to exclude light and removed when we wish to see how the worms have been burrowing. Worms are light-sensitive and burrow away from the light. If the cover is not put over the wormery, the worms will keep to the centre of the soil and their burrows will not be seen.

Purchased or constructed wormeries

These are filled in the same way as the sweet jar. Much less soil will be needed. Provide a black paper cover over the clear plastic for the reason discussed above. Make sure the soil is damp at all times.

Activity

The worms are placed on top of the soil in the wormery. To encourage them to start burrowing, a small amount of damp soil should be sprinkled over them.

Each day the black paper cover should be removed and the burrows observed. It is surprising how quickly the layers of sand and soil become mixed due to the worms' burrowing. In his book *Earthworms*, Charles Darwin describes how he calculated the effects of this burrowing.

The dampness of the soil should be checked daily as well as last thing on Friday afternoon and first thing on Monday morning. The soil should be damp but not waterlogged. Do not keep the worms for longer than two to three weeks.

Recording

The children could draw their wormery in their notebook and describe how they prepared it for the worms. This could be followed up by writing and drawing about their observations on the worms' burrowing. These daily observations can be combined with those suggested for the next Activity.

Activity 43   WHAT DO WORMS EAT?

Aim

To encourage careful observation.

Equipment

As for Activity 42.

Activity

The children should cut the various foods into cubes using knives, borrowed, perhaps, from the school kitchen (not sharp knives). The reason for the cubic shape is that the worms will feed at the corners and angles of the cubes: it will therefore be possible to see which foods the worms prefer. The worms will eat some leaves but they also pull the leaves down into their burrows without eating them. It is thought that the leaves are used to cover the openings of burrows in this way either to stop rain entering or to discourage predatory animals.

Recording

The children could draw the cubes of food before and after they have been given to the worms and could follow this with their observations and conclusions.

Activity 44   CAN WORMS SMELL?

Aim

To give the children experience of a simple Activity to test the reaction of a worm to a particular scent or odour.
To emphasise again to the children how we must treat worms with care and consideration.

Activity

The worms must be kept damp: they breathe through their skin and can only breathe if their skin is covered with a fine film of water. They should only be used in this Activity for a few minutes.

It is advisable for the teacher to provide extra worms for this Activity, otherwise it will mean that the children have to dismantle their wormeries.

Only a small pad of cotton wool is needed with about two drops of the essence. The pad should be brought very slowly towards the worm from about thirty centimetres away. The closest it should be to the worm is about five centimetres. This Activity should be carried out in shady conditions: if the worms are in bright light they will wriggle around trying to get away from the light. It is then very difficult to determine whether the worm is reacting to the light or to the scent.

Other essences could be used as well as or instead of the peppermint suggested.

Recording

The children could describe what they did and what they found out. We should be careful in this type of work to see that the children do not jump to conclusions too quickly or with insufficient evidence. In their writing we should encourage them to say, 'Worms do not seem to like . . .' rather than, 'Worms do not like . . .'.

Activity 45   MORE ABOUT WORMS

Aim

To give the children practice in careful observation.

Equipment

The purpose of the sheet of paper suggested in the Pupils' Book is so that the worms make a noise with their bristles when they wriggle around. The hand lens does not need to be an expensive one: the plastic hand lenses available from suppliers or from stationery shops are quite suitable for this work.

Activity

1   The worm is placed on the sheet of paper and allowed to wriggle around. As it does so it will make a sound rather like that heard when sandpaper is being used. If the worm is then carefully lifted up and turned over, the bristles (in pairs on each segment of the body) can be seen with a hand lens.

2   This part of the Activity is a question which the children have to find their own way of answering. A suitable sound source is two spoons which are tapped together.

3   To answer this question the children could use small torches which they bring towards the worm to test its reaction to the bright light.

When the children have completed their tests the worms should quickly be put back into a box of damp soil in a cool place.

Recording

The children could write about what they did and what they found out. Many children may find it easier to describe what they did by using a series of drawings.

Activity 46   LOOKING FOR SNAILS

Aim

To let the children look for snails, collect snails and bring them back into the classroom for more detailed study.
To let the children observe the habitats in which snails live.

Equipment

The boxes of damp soil can be those used for collecting the worms in Activity 41.

Activity

It is essential to look for possible sources of snails beforehand. The school grounds or the local park or open space will usually provide a large enough supply. Some teachers may prefer to collect the snails themselves before the lesson. This Activity can then be omitted. Visits outside school do take up a considerable amount of time. On the other hand, finding the snails in their natural habitat is a valuable lesson in itself.

Providing the weather has not been hot and dry, snails are quite easy to find. They can be found under stones and rocks, under pieces of wood, under rotting leaves, anywhere in fact that is damp and dark.

Two snails per group will be sufficient.

Remember to tell the children to note down where they found their snails so that, at the end of their work with the snails, they can be returned to their original environment.

Recording

If the children found the snails themselves, they should write about their search for snails and describe where they found them.

Activity 47 A HOME FOR SNAILS

Aim

To demonstrate to the children that they have a responsibility to the living things they have brought into the classroom. Their main responsibility here is to provide a home and food for the snails.

Equipment

A plastic box such as a 2kg margarine tub is suitable. A plastic aquarium is better. These are reasonably cheap and very useful.

Activity

The damp soil is placed in the container. It should be about 10cm deep if using a plastic aquarium but about 4cm deep if using a plastic margarine box. The tufts of grass (including the roots) should be planted in the soil. The stones should be arranged so that they provide shelter for the snails. A lid should be put over the top of the aquarium. The lid should be supported by small blobs of plasticine to provide ventilation. Make sure the snails are kept cool and away from direct sunlight.

Feeding the snails is quite easy: give them almost any green food. They particularly like lettuce leaves or the leaves from French marigolds or African marigolds, two plants frequently grown in gardens.

Recording

The children could write about how they set up the snails' home. They could also keep records of their observations on the snails.

Activity 48 LOOKING AT SNAILS

Aim

The primary aim is to give children practice in accurate observation – the children will look carefully at a snail and see the external structure.

Equipment

The sheet of clear plastic should be about 20cm square and about 3mm thick. Plastic of this sort can be purchased from D.I.Y. shops: it is used in some forms of double glazing. It can be cut with a fine-toothed saw. It can also be scored with a sharp craft knife and then snapped along the score line. Do this carefully as the edges can be very sharp. Rub down the cut edges with sandpaper.

Activity

The snail is placed foot downwards on the plastic, which should have been moistened. In a short time it will put out its foot and its head. It is important that the snail is not disturbed: it will contract back into its shell and take even longer to stretch out again. The snail has four 'horns' or tentacles. The longer pair have light receptors or eyes at the top. The shorter pair are for smelling.

The children should carefully lift up the plastic so that they can see the undersurface of the snail's foot. They should be able to see the bands of muscle across the foot and the mouth near the front end of the foot.

Recording

The children could draw the snail as they see it from above and from below the sheet of plastic. They can label the foot, shell, horns or tentacles, and mouth.

If the snail moves across the plastic on the desk the children can measure how far it moves in one minute.

Activity 49   HOW DOES A SNAIL FEED?

Aim

To give the children further practice in observation.

Equipment

The sheet of plastic can be that used for the previous Activity. If these two Activities are to be carried out during the same lesson, each group must be provided with two pieces of plastic sheeting.

Before the lesson the sheet of plastic should be coated with a thin layer of flour and water paste. The paste should be made by mixing a small amount of flour with water. Do not make it too thick. Spread the paste over the plastic with cotton wool or a cloth and leave it to dry.

Activity

The snail is carefully placed on the paste-coated plastic. As it extends its foot and senses the flour it will usually begin to feed. It scrapes off the flour with its radula which is rather like a tongue. When it has cleared the flour from one area it will move forward.

Recording

The children could draw the snail as it appears from under the plastic as it is feeding. They could also write a few sentences describing what happened and what they saw.

Activity 50   WHAT DO SNAILS EAT?

Aim

To give the children experience of testing the response of an animal in a 'choice' situation.

Activity

The food is placed in a circle about 15cm across. The snail is placed in the middle of the circle and its movement observed.

If time allows the snails could be placed with different foods directly in front of them: they may not be able to sense the foods behind them. Other snails can also be tested to see if their reactions are similar.

Recording

The children could describe what they did and what they found out.

Activity 51   THE SNAIL'S SENSES

Aim

To let the children test a snail to find out about its senses.

Activity

1 Can the snail smell?

The snail is placed on a flat surface and allowed to emerge from its shell. A small piece of orange peel is first squeezed and then brought up slowly towards the snail, but without touching it. Start from about 35cm away. The snail is watched carefully for any reaction. Snails do not 'like' the smell of orange and withdraw their horns when they have sensed the smell. Other snails can be tested to find out if they all react in the same way at the same distance.

2 Does the snail like light?

A lighted torch is gradually brought up to a snail which has come out of its shell and its reaction noted. If possible this part of the Activity should be carried out in a dimly-lit part of the classroom.

3 Can the snail hear?

The two spoons are banged together at varying distances from the snail and the snail's reactions noted.

4 Can the snail feel?

The most important words in the Pupils' Book are 'blunt' and 'gently'. It is essential that the children treat the animals carefully.

Introduction

In the Energy section of Pupils' Book 1A the concept of energy was introduced. In the Energy section of Book 1B we are consolidating these introductory ideas by considering energy 'in action' and looking at sound energy. Here the result of energy being put into a device or a system is that we hear sounds. For example, if we use energy to force air through a recorder, the air issues from the holes in such a way that our ear drums are made to vibrate. The end result is that our brain recognises sound. Similarly, if we use energy to rub a piece of sandpaper over a piece of wood which we are trying to smooth down, the energy will eventually finish up in the molecules of the sandpaper and the wood. This causes the molecules to vibrate more rapidly. We recognise this extra vibration by the fact that the sandpaper and the wood feel hotter.

So, depending on how energy is used, we get different results. It can be used to produce heat and light from an electric light bulb, to make a crane lift a load, or to make a recorder produce sounds.

While working through these Activities with the children it is very important for us to bear in mind that it is energy we are dealing with. Recorders do not produce sounds by themselves: air has to be forcibly pushed through the recorder before sounds are produced. In other words, work has to be done on the air passing through the recorder before sounds are produced.

The Activities in this section could be carried out in a circus type of organisation. If the equipment for each of the five Activities is prepared in duplicate, there will be sufficient equipment for ten groups. As the Activities do not all need the same amount of time, it is suggested that there is sufficient equipment available at the beginning for all groups to make, for example, the string telephone. Then, if there is a hold-up in the circus, a group can carry on with the string telephone while another group is completing the next Activity.

Activity 52   WAYS OF MAKING SOUNDS

Aim

To introduce to the children the idea that sound is always produced by movement of some sort. So, to produce a sound, energy must be used.

Equipment

The equipment needed will depend very much on how the Activity is carried out. If carried out as suggested in the Pupils' Book, it is a 'paper activity' and no equipment is required. However, some teachers may prefer to carry out this Activity in a more practical manner. In this case the children would not only think of ways of making sounds, but would actually make them. If the teacher decides to do this and it is the best way (but not the quietest!) then a variety of objects must be available. These objects could include a comb and paper, a hammer, spoons,

recorders, rubber bands and castanets. Many children will require a visual stimulus (partly provided by the drawings on page 26) to get their minds working on other ways of making sounds.

For each way of making a sound ask yourself:
What would I have to do to make the sound?

In your notebook write down all the ways you
thought of to make a sound.
Did other children in your class find other ways?

To make a sound something has to move.
When you clap your hands, you have to move your
hands together.
When you speak, you have to move air through
your voice box and out through your mouth.
When you pluck an elastic band, you have to pull
the band and then let it go.

page 27

Recording

The children could describe with drawings the different ways they found to make sounds. The question on page 27 should be discussed. Then, for each of the ways they found to make a sound, the children should write down what they had to do to make the sound.

Follow-up

This Activity could obviously be tied in with work done in music lessons. Many primary schools have a selection of musical instruments and these could be used to consolidate the point that to produce any sound, movement must occur.

Activity 53 A STRING TELEPHONE

Aim

To let the children find out that sound can be transmitted through a length of string.

Equipment

Plastic drinking cups are particularly suitable for this Activity. The holes in the bottom of the cups are best made with the point of a steel knitting needle which has been heated. If the string is glued to the bottom of the cup after being tied to the matchstick, the telephone will work better. Make the length of string between the telephones at least 8-10 metres, otherwise it is rather pointless using the telephone.

If the children use the telephone in a corridor, they could be asked to find out what happens if the telephone line has to go round a corner. If it touches the wall, the vibration will be stopped and the telephone will not work.

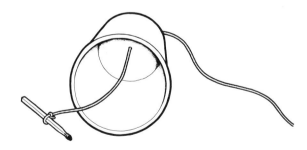

Recording

In their notebooks the children could make a drawing to show the telephone in use. They could then write about how they made and used the telephone. Some of the children may need help when they write about how the telephone works.

Activity 54   LISTENING TO OURSELVES

Aim
To let the children find out how sound can be transmitted through the air in a stethoscope.

Equipment
The model stethoscope is quite easy to make and full details are given in the construction notes.

Activity
As the stethoscope has to be held over the user's ears, the children must work in groups. The children should be able to hear a heartbeat and also the sounds of breathing.

Recording
This could be in the form of a drawing of the stethoscope together with some writing about how they used it and how they think it works.

Activity 55   HEARING THROUGH WOOD

Aim
To show children that sound travels even better through wood than through air.

Recording
The children could write about what they did and what happened. They could also try to describe what this Activity shows them.

Activity 56   A PAPER FLUTE

Aim

To get the children to make a paper flute and then to investigate what happens when the design is varied.

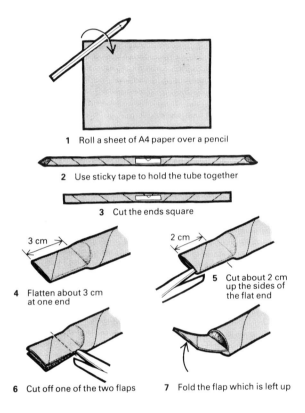

1   Roll a sheet of A4 paper over a pencil

2   Use sticky tape to hold the tube together

3   Cut the ends square

3 cm

4   Flatten about 3 cm at one end

2 cm

5   Cut about 2 cm up the sides of the flat end

6   Cut off one of the two flaps

7   Fold the flap which is left up

Equipment

A4 paper is needed to make the flute. For economy, the A4 sheets could be cut in half across the long edge. This size paper will still make a satisfactory flute.

Besides scissors, the only other equipment needed is some sticky tape.

Activity

You may have to remind the children that air has to be *sucked* through to make the flute work. The main difficulty children come across in making the flute is in cutting the vibrating part. The flute is flattened for about three centimetres at one end. Two cuts are then made up the creases for about two centimetres. This produces two flaps. One of these flaps is cut off across the flute. The other flap is folded up to cover the open end of the tube. As air is sucked up the flute it is this flap which vibrates and so produces the sound in the tube.

The children should be reminded about hygiene: each person's flute should not be used by anybody else in the class.

Recording

The children could describe with words and drawings how they made the flute. They could also describe what happened when they made a longer, shorter, fatter or thinner flute.

Introduction

One of the most important aims of our work in science in the primary school is to open our pupils' eyes to the wonders of the world in which they live. The living world is fascinating to children and if we can help them to learn how to observe and find out about the plants and animals around them, we may start a life-long interest.

Animals, because they move about and because they are like us in many ways, are immediately interesting to children. Plants are basically static organisms and children are liable to accept them as just a part of the environment.

Through our work in school we can show that plants can be just as interesting as animals and that they are worthwhile objects of study. Children show great delight when they see seeds they have planted starting to grow, or when they see buds opening in the spring.

One problem when tackling biological work with children is that of identification and naming. In this section children will be looking at trees in general and one tree in particular. They should know the name of the tree they are studying. Identification has been made as simple as possible: two Mastersheets are provided with drawings of the leaves of sixteen of the more common trees. However, although the problem of identification has been overcome here, it is not so easy to solve in later work. We should not overemphasise identification but should point out to the children that it is sometimes necessary to distinguish one sort of plant from another. To do this we give each individual species a particular name.

It was decided to start the work on plants with a look at trees for a number of reasons. Trees are common even in industrial areas. All towns and cities have parks and open spaces and many of the parks have an excellent collection of trees. Many suburban and rural schools are lucky enough to have trees in their grounds. Trees are large plants which are quite easy to identify. They are also very beautiful at all times of the year and play a very important part in the appearance of our environment.

It is assumed that this work will be tackled during the summer term – June is a very good month as many deciduous trees are in full leaf and, in early June, may be displaying their flowers.

If possible the groups within a particular class should study different trees. If the work of all the groups is displayed, the children will be able to learn about a variety of common trees. No distinction has been made in this section between deciduous and evergreen trees, but it is advisable for the children to look, initially at least, at deciduous trees. The identification of many coniferous trees is quite difficult and many are not native to Britain.

Before starting this section, it is a good idea to survey the area around the school to see where suitable trees are sited. The children must be able to get close to the tree (for bark rubbings, trunk measurements, etc) and yet be able to view the full height of the tree. It is as well if the teacher identifies the trees before the children start their work.

If this study entails leaving the school and going to the local park, try to plan the work carefully so that the time spent on the visit is justified. At all times the importance of treating trees with care and respect should be impressed upon the children. Pulling twigs from trees and cutting off pieces of bark are practices which not only harm the tree, but also spoil the appearance of the tree and thus the environment as a whole.

Activity 57   WHAT SORT OF TREE?

Aim

To demonstrate to the children that there are many different sorts of trees.
To show the children one method of identifying a tree: by leaf shape.

Equipment

Each child needs a leaf from his or her tree. These leaves may be found under the tree or they can be carefully picked from a part of the tree where the least harm will be done. Breaking off branches to get a leaf or two is to be strongly discouraged.

Mastersheet

Each child will require a copy of Mastersheets 28 and 29.

Activity

The drawing of the leaf can be made as soon as the children return to the classroom after selecting their tree. Many children of this age find it very difficult to draw the shape they see freehand. However, as suggested in the Pupils' Book, they could draw round the leaf while it is firmly held down.

Recording

The teacher may decide that this tree work could be kept in a separate tree folder or book. The work described in this section could well extend into the Autumn and Spring Terms so that the life of the tree is observed throughout the full year.

For this Activity the children put the two Mastersheets into their books or folders together with the named drawing of the leaf from their tree. They could also write down where their tree is situated.

Activity 58   HOW BIG IS THE LEAF?

Aim

To emphasise the fact that leaves are, in general, very thin, but have a comparatively large surface area.

This Activity could be used as an introduction to area measurement.

Equipment

The centimetre-squared paper can be copied from Mastersheet G/4.

Activity

The children first carefully draw round the leaf on the squared paper. Then all the complete squares inside the drawing are marked off and counted. Next the incomplete squares are counted: the children have to judge whether more or less than half a square is included within the leaf's outline. If more than half, then this is counted as a full square. If less than half, then the square is not counted. If the children doubt this method of finding the surface area, suggest that they draw round the leaf a second time, placing the leaf in a different position on the paper. They will find that the number of centimetre squares in the outline of the leaf is the same or only varies by one square either way.

Recording

The squared paper with the leaf drawing(s) could be put in the folder or notebook. A short written explanation could accompany the drawing(s).

Activity 59 MAKING A PLASTER CAST OF A LEAF

Aim

To give the children practice in the technique of making a plaster cast.
To get the children to look at the colour and venation of the leaf. To get them to mix a paint which is as near the green of the leaf as possible.

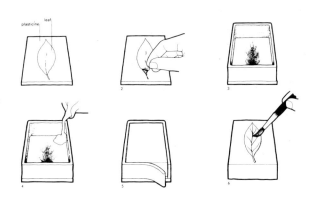

Equipment

As a considerable amount of plasticine is needed to make the moulds, particularly for the larger leaves, it may be necessary to spread this Activity over a period of time. In addition, it is probably better not to have too many groups mixing plaster of Paris at the same time: it tends to be a rather messy (but very worthwhile) Activity.

The best plaster to use can be obtained from a local chemist or from suppliers such as Griffin and George or Philip Harris. It is usually called 'dental plaster'. Ordinary building plaster is too coarse for this work. Modelling plaster is also very good but can be expensive. Firms which supply materials for making such things as plaster cast chess sets will often have fine plaster suitable for this work.

Activity

The working area should be covered with a polythene sheet or newspaper. The children should wear aprons or other protective clothing.

The plasticine is rolled into a flat shape about 7-10mm thick. The best tool for this job is a rolling pin, a bottle or a thick piece of dowel rod. A rectangle is cut from the flat sheet. The rectangle needs to be about 1cm wider than the leaf all round. Plastic knives are very suitable and quite safe to use for this.

The leaf is now placed on the rectangle of plasticine and pressed into it. A flat piece of wood or thick cardboard is useful here. Try to get the children to press evenly over the whole area of the leaf. The leaf is then carefully removed. Now a wall about 2cm high is built up round the four sides of the rectangle. The wall should make a good seal with the base, otherwise the plaster will leak out.

When mixing the plaster two mistakes are commonly made:

1 putting in too much plaster, which makes the plaster/water mixture too thick.
2 mixing too much plaster.

To avoid these mistakes, use the following method:

1 Nearly fill the mould with water.
2 Pour the water into the mixing bowl.
3 Add plaster *without mixing* until there is just a film of water over the plaster.
4 Stir with the spoon.
5 When the mixture is smooth and about the consistency of double cream, pour it into the mould.
6 Tap the table and the mould a few times to displace air bubbles.
7 Leave to set, preferably overnight. If this is not possible, leave for at least an hour in a warm room.
8 Remove the walls from the mould.
9 Peel the plasticine from the plaster. Do this very carefully as the plaster will still be quite fragile.
10 Leave for at least a day before painting.
11 Put a label on the cast.

Before painting, the plaster can be sealed. If this is not done the paint will be absorbed by the plaster. The easiest method is to brush the plaster with wallpaper paste. Be very careful if the paste contains a fungicide as this is poisonous. It is better to use a paste which does not contain fungicide.

Recording

The children could make a display of their finished casts. They will then be able to see those made by other groups. They could also write in their notebooks about the way they made their casts.

Activity 60 MAKING A BARK RUBBING

Aim

To introduce the children to this technique. To let the children discover that a particular pattern is common to one sort of tree.

Equipment

Heel ball is the substance used by shoe menders to colour the new leather used in repairing shoes. Some shoe menders will sell heel ball. Otherwise it can be obtained from a craft shop or supplier. Wax crayons, particularly the 'giant' size are also suitable.

The paper used should be strong but not too thick.

Activity

At the first attempt many children will tear the paper by rubbing too hard with the heel ball, but they quickly learn how much pressure to apply. It is a good idea for the teacher to demonstrate the technique. In this case the teacher should try it out beforehand.

Recording

A few short sentences describing the method used to make the bark rubbing could be put in their notebooks to accompany the bark rubbing.

Follow-up

This technique can be used to make rubbings of many other items. The rubbings taken from manhole covers or the brass plates in churches are examples. The rubbings taken from blocks of wood with pronounced grain are also interesting. These rubbings can be made across or with the grain of the wood.

Activity 61 MEASURING YOUR TREE TRUNK

Aim

To give the children practice in measuring and to familiarise them with centimetres and metres.

Equipment

The measuring tape can be the one made up from Mastersheet G/5. Make sure each group has a long enough length of string. It is better to give each group a small ball of string.

Recording

The children could describe how they measured the distance round the trunk of the tree. They could make a record of the distance round their tree and also those round the other trees measured by other groups.

Activity 62   HOW HIGH IS YOUR TREE?

Aim
To introduce the children to a method of estimating the height of a tree.

Equipment
The stick should be about 30cm long. If sticks are not available, strips of thick card could be used.

Activity
What we are trying to do here is to find out how many times the tree is taller than the child standing next to the tree. Suggest to the children that they try to find points of reference up the tree. For example, they might find that the first branch up the tree corresponds with twice the height of the child. This, then, becomes the references point for the 'feet' of the child for measuring the third height up the tree, and so on.

Recording
The children could describe in writing and drawings how they found the height of their tree.

Follow-up
Using the same method the children could find the height of the tallest tree they can find. They could also find out if their tree is as tall or taller than the school building or a nearby church, etc.

Activity 63   THE TREE'S UMBRELLA

Aim
To give the children practice in measuring length.
To bring to the children's attention the fact that many trees cut out most of the sunlight from the ground below them. This inhibits the growth of other plants under the trees.

Equipment
It would be preferable for the children to use either the metre sticks used in the Energy 1 section of Book 1A or a cloth tape measure.

Activity
The children should work in pairs. One child should direct the other child as to where the

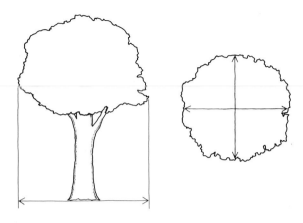

'umbrella' starts and finishes: this child stands away from the tree so that he or she can easily see the extent of the 'umbrella'.

Recording

The children could draw out the shape of their tree's 'umbrella' and put on their drawing the measurements they made. They should also write in the answers to the questions at the bottom of page 41 of the Pupils' Book.

Follow-up

As mentioned previously this tree study could extend into the Autumn and Spring Terms.

Introduction

To most children light is noticed more by its absence than by its presence: many children are afraid of the dark.

Light energy is produced in the form of waves. The light waves can have different wavelengths. These wavelengths are sensed by the retina of the eye as different colours. Long wavelengths are at the red end of the spectrum while the shorter wavelengths are at the violet end of the spectrum.

In the primary school light can best be studied by looking at what we can do with light: make shadows, reflect it with mirrors, refract it with lenses and prisms, and disperse it into its component colours.

In this introductory section we are going to consolidate and follow up the work started on shadows in the Time section of Book 1A. The Activities in this section are concerned with what happens if we put an object in the path of a beam of light – the light is stopped and a dark area is produced. This is a shadow. A clear, sharp shadow is produced when no light or very little light reaches the area in shadow. A perfect shadow is seen as a black area (no light) but most shadows are grey due to some light reaching the shadowed area.

Towards the end of the section two Activities are included which look at the way plane (flat) mirrors reflect a beam of light.

Pages 42 and 43 in the Pupils' Book are designed to make the children think about the importance of light. We need light and receptors (our eyes) to see what is around us. This leads us to consider the various sources of light. Natural light comes to us from the Sun and the Moon (reflected sunlight). If the Sun's light is obscured by heavy clouds during the day, and at night-time, we have ways of producing light energy artificially. An interesting point here is that the light energy from the artificial sources is really the energy from sunlight being released after millions of years. Sunlight was trapped by green plants living on the Earth at that time. These plants eventually became the coal and oil which we now use to fire our power stations. The natural gas which is used extensively for producing power is the result of the partial decomposition of plant and animal remains.

Activity 64   LOOKING AT OUR SHADOWS

Aim

To emphasise to the children the fact that shadows are formed when an object interrupts the path of a beam of light.
To introduce the idea that for a shadow to be produced, three conditions are essential:
1 a source of light
2 an object interrupting the path of this light
3 a surface on which the shadow can fall.

Mastersheet

Each child will require a copy of Mastersheet 30.

Recording

When the children have returned to the classroom and discussed their findings, they

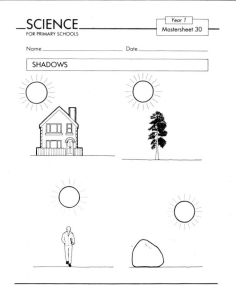

should be given Mastersheet 30. The simple drawings on this Mastersheet should be completed by the children to show where shadows would be produced. By looking at the Mastersheets after the children have completed the drawings, we can get a good idea as to whether they understand how shadows are produced.

Activity 65   SHADOWS IN THE CLASSROOM

Aim
As for Activity 64.

Equipment
A screen is easily made by fixing a sheet of white paper to the classroom wall. If this is not possible, a sheet of white card, at least 30cm by 30cm, could be supported by wooden blocks or piles of books. The support stands used in the Structures section of Book 1A could also be used here.

The torches should be quite large: the batteries in small torches will be quickly discharged in the classroom. (Note: now that rechargeable batteries are available, schools would be well advised to invest in a charger and a supply of rechargeable batteries. The initial expenditure is high but this will be quickly offset by the savings made.)

Activity
The torch could be supported on a wooden block and held in place with plasticine or sticky tape.

By moving their hand towards and away from the screen the children will see that the sharpest and clearest shadows are produced when their hand is quite close to the screen.

Recording
As suggested in the Pupils' Book, the children could make drawings to show how they made the shadows. They could also write a short description of how they made various shapes of shadows on the screen.

They should also write down their answer to the question: 'We need 3 things to make a shadow. What are they?'

Activity 66   SHADOW PICTURES

Aim
To let the children make silhouette pictures. To give the children practice in the skills of drawing round a shape and cutting out using scissors.

Activity
To get a sharp shadow the child needs to sit with his or her head fairly close to the paper. Some adjustment of the position of the torch may be necessary before a really good shadow is produced.

Recording
The mounted silhouette could be fixed in the children's notebooks. Before this is done, however, a classroom display of the unlabelled silhouettes can be interesting. Can we tell to whom each silhouette belongs?

Activity 67   A SHADOW THEATRE

Aim

To give the children further practical experience of forming shadows.

Equipment

The shadow theatre can be made from thick cardboard or from plywood. The construction of the plywood theatre is described in the construction notes. If using thick card, similar measurements can be used.

Activity

The children could start by cutting out simple shapes such as the house shown on page 46 of the Pupils' Book. This will give them an idea of how the shadow theatre works. They can then go on to make trees, people, animals, etc.

Follow-up

This work with the shadow theatre could lead to the writing and performing of simple shadow plays. Some children get very interested in this work and it can lead to some valuable creative writing.

Activity 68   BOUNCING LIGHT

Aim

To introduce the children to the reflection of a light beam by a mirror, so that they can see that the light is reflected in a certain way.

Equipment

The mirrors used should be at least 7.5cm square. For safety and ease of handling, the mirrors can be mounted on pieces of wood as described in the construction notes.

Activity

If the beam of light from the torch meets the mirror head-on (that is at right angles), then the light will be reflected back in the direction from which it came.

If either the torch or the mirror is moved so that the light beam does not meet the mirror at right angles, the beam of light will be reflected at an angle to the mirror which is the same as the angle at which the beam hits the mirror.

By trying to make the beam of light hit the ceiling and then the four walls of the classroom, the children will find out that the beam of light is always reflected in the same plane. That is to say, the beam of light hitting the mirror and the beam reflected from the mirror lie on the same (imaginary) flat surface.

Note

It should be pointed out to the children how dangerous it is to reflect beams of light, particularly sunlight, into a person's eyes.

Recording

The children could write about what they did and what they discovered, using drawings.

Activity 69   BOUNCING LIGHT WITH 2 MIRRORS

Aim

As in the previous Activity.

Equipment

As Activity 68, except that each group will need two mirrors and a screen. The screens can be those used for Activity 65.

Activity

From the previous Activity the children should know that for a beam of light from the torch to be reflected on to another mirror they will have to turn the mirror at an angle to the incoming beam.

The mirrors and screen should be fairly close to one another if the classroom is well lit.

Recording

The children could make a record of what they did and what happened.

Construction notes

Egyptian sunbar

1 Cut a 30cm length of 50mm × 25mm wood.
2 Cut a piece of 6mm plywood to this shape:

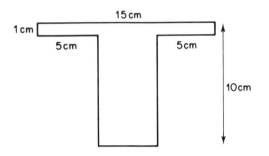

3 Glue and pin the plywood shape to one end of the 50mm × 25mm wood.

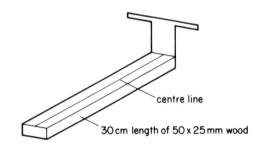

4 Mark in the centre line.

Stirring rod

1 Cut 3mm or 6mm dowel rod into 20cm lengths. 3mm dowel is not normally stocked by timber yards but it can often be obtained from model shops.
2 Sand both ends round.
3 Give each rod at least 3 coats of polyurethane varnish. Allow at least 12 hours between coats.

Metre stick

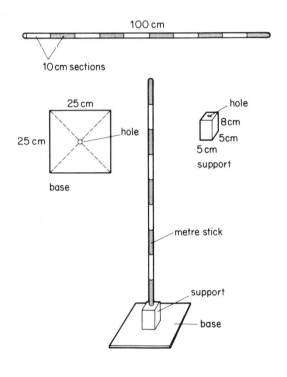

1 Cut the base of the stand from 9mm plywood. It should be 25cm by 25cm.
2 Cut the support from 50mm by 50mm wood. The support should be 8cm high.
3 Sand both pieces of wood smooth.
4 Cut a metre length of 9mm dowel. Paint it with primer/sealer. When dry, mark off in 10cm lengths. Paint alternate sections red. When dry paint the remaining sections white.
5 Drill a vertical hole through the 8cm support: the size of the hole should be such that the painted metre stick will just fit in the hole.
6 Drill a similar sized hole in the middle of the base.
7 Carefully matching the hole in the base with the hole in the support, glue and pin the base and the support together.

Ramp and adjustable support

Ramp

1 Cut a 100cm length from 15cm wide, 12mm thick, melamine-surfaced chipboard. This is sold under various trade names of which 'Contiboard' is probably the best known.
2 Cut two 100cm lengths of 25mm by 6mm wood.
3 Glue and pin these to the sides of the Contiboard.

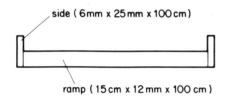

side (6mm x 25mm x 100cm)

ramp (15cm x 12mm x 100cm)

4 Screw in two cup hooks at one end of the ramp. They should be about 4cm in from each edge.

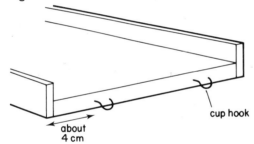

cup hook

about 4 cm

Support

1 Cut two 35cm lengths of 50mm by 25mm wood.

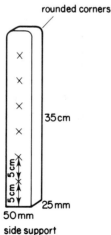

rounded corners

35cm

5cm 5cm 5cm

25mm

50mm

side support

2 Mark the positions of the holes as shown in the drawing. These need to be marked on one piece only: the holes can be drilled with the two pieces of wood clamped together. In this way the two sets of holes will match each other exactly. The holes should be of such a size that the dowel rod you are using is a tight fit. The dowel rod can be either 6mm or 9mm diameter. Cut six lengths of this dowel 22cm long.
3 Cut the base from 9mm plywood.
4 In the middle of the two long sides of the base cut out pieces which are exactly the same size (or very slightly smaller for a really tight fit) as the two side supports. Sand the base down thoroughly.

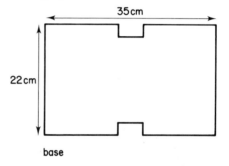

35cm

22cm

base

5 Glue the dowels into the holes in the side supports.
6 Mount the side supports on the base.
7 For strengtheners, cut two 8cm squares of 9mm plywood.
8 Cut these across the diagonal.
9 Glue these between the side supports and the base.

8 cm

8cm

strengthener

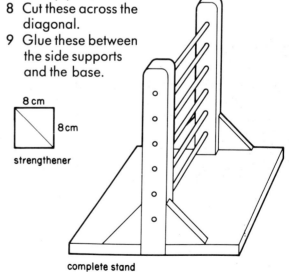

complete stand

Feelie box

1 Using 9mm plywood, cut out the following
   pieces:

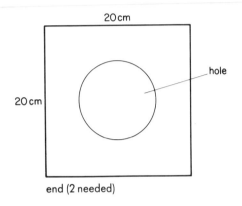

end (2 needed)

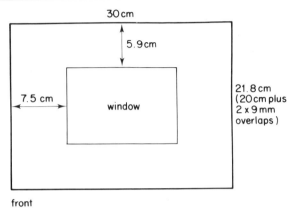

front

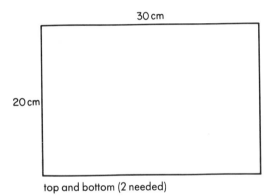

top and bottom (2 needed)

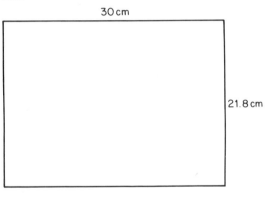

back

2 From the ends cut out circles of about 5cm
   radius: these are to put the hands through.
3 From the front cut out the window opening.
4 Cut a piece of 3mm clear plastic 1cm wider
   all round than the window opening. For the
   window shown, this plastic will be 12cm by
   17cm.
5 Cut two circles of 7cm radius from fairly
   thick black polythene.
6 From the centres of the polythene circles,
   make a series of radial cuts which finish
   about 2cm from the circumference.
7 Glue these circles in place, inside the ends.
8 Glue and pin the top and bottom to the ends.
9 Glue and pin the front and back in place.
10 Paint or varnish to give a good finish.

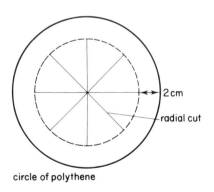

circle of polythene

Mystery Box

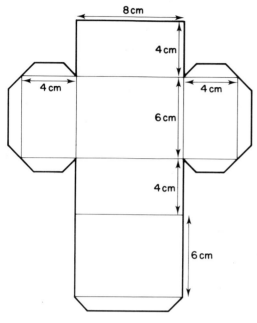

Tabs about 1cm deep.
The size is not critical.
This size fits on A4 card.

1 Mark out the net on a piece of A4 card.
2 Score the fold lines.
3 Cut out and fold to shape.
4 Glue the long tab and one side.
5 Put in the 'mystery' items and then glue the open side in place.
6 Number the box and write down its contents on a separate piece of paper or card.

Support stand

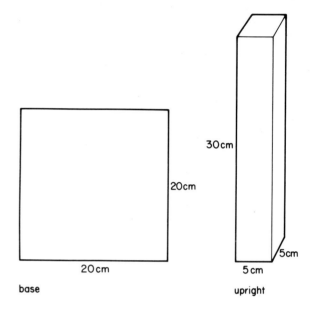

base

upright

1 Cut the base from 9mm plywood.
2 Cut the upright from 50mm by 50mm wood.
3 Glue and screw the upright in the middle of the base.

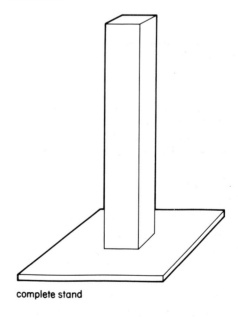

complete stand

Wormery

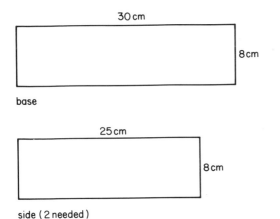

base

side (2 needed)

1 Cut the base and sides from 9mm plywood.
2 Cut four 25cm lengths of 6mm by 6mm wood.
3 Glue and pin these to the sides:

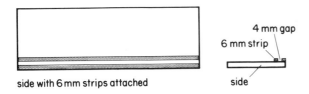

side with 6mm strips attached   side

4 Cut two 27cm lengths of 6mm square wood.
5 Glue and pin these to the base:

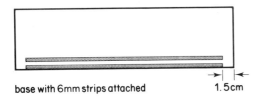

base with 6mm strips attached   1.5cm

6 Glue and pin the base to the two sides. The groove made by the 6mm square wood should match up round the three sides.
7 Cut a piece of 3mm plywood to fit the back: take the measurements from the structure you have already made.
8 Glue and pin the back in place.
9 Now cut a piece of 3mm clear plastic (acrylic) to fit into the grooves to make the clear front.

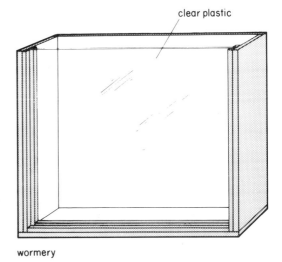

wormery

Stethoscope

1 You will need: 3 plastic funnels about 10cm across, a T-piece and about a metre of plastic tubing. The T-piece must be a tight fit with the plastic tubing.
2 Cut the tubing into 3 lengths: two 40cm long and one 20cm long. (These lengths are not critical: they can be altered to suit the size of the children using the stethoscope.)
3 If the tubing will not fit either into or on to the stem of the funnels, the stems can be cut to make the tubing fit.
4 Fit the stethoscope together:

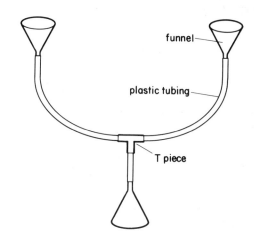

Shadow theatre

1 Glue and pin the top and bottom to the sides of the base.
2 Glue and pin the back of the base in place.
3 Finally glue and pin the front in place.
4 Paint with primer/sealer.
5 Give two coats of gloss paint.
6 Cut out a piece of tracing paper 32cm by 24.5cm.
7 Glue this in place behind the opening in the front.
8 Smooth out the screen before the glue dries.

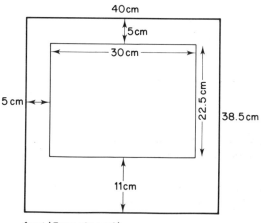

front (3mm plywood)

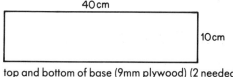

top and bottom of base (9mm plywood) (2 needed)

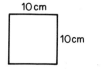

side (9mm plywood) (2 needed)

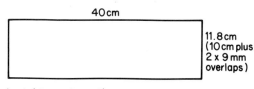

back (9mm plywood)

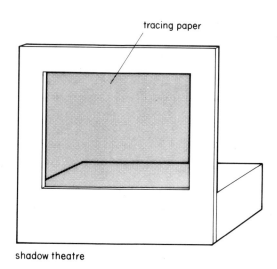

shadow theatre

Mounted mirror

1 You will need a mirror tile from a D.I.Y. shop.
They are made in various sizes but the size I
have found most convenient is 11cm square.
2 Cut two pieces of 9mm or 12mm plywood very
slightly (1mm) larger than the mirror.

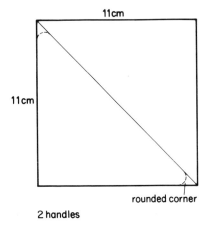

2 handles

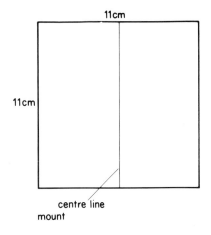

3 Cut one square across the diagonal: this
makes two handles. Round off the corners as
shown. (You only need one of these handles
per mirror.)
4 Mark in the centre line on both sides of the
mirror mount.
5 Glue and pin the handle in place using the
centre lines as guides.
6 Make sure the mirror mount and the handle
line up so that the mirror will stand at right
angles to the surface on which it is placed.
7 Paint the mirror handle and mount.
8 Mount the mirror using the fixing pads on the
mirror.

Suppliers

1   Primary Science Apparatus
    2 Lapwing Close
    Grovehill
    Hemel Hempstead
    Herts HP2 6DS

2   Griffin and George Ltd
    285 Ealing Road
    Alperton
    HA0 1HJ

3   Philip Harris Ltd
    Lynn Lane
    Shenstone
    Staffordshire WS14 0EE

4   Hestair Hope Ltd
    St Philip's Drive
    Royton
    Oldham OL2 6AG

5   ESA/E.J. Arnold
    Parkside Lane
    Densbury Road
    Leeds LS11 5TD

6   E S Perry Ltd
    Osmiroid Works
    104 Fareham Road
    Gosport
    Hampshire PO13 0AL

Bibliography

Science 5/13
   With Objectives in Mind
   Early Experiences
   Learning Through Science
   Time
   Structures and Forces
   Science and Toys
   Science Resources for Primary and Middle
      Schools
   Ourselves
   Minibeasts
Science for Children with Learning Difficulties
All published by Macdonald Educational for the
Schools Council.

Practical Primary Science, Romola Showell,
Ward Lock Educational (1983)

*The Teaching of Primary Science: Policy and
Practice,* edited by Colin Richards and Derek
Holford, The Falmer Press (1983)

Teaching Science to Infants, Romola Showell,
Ward Lock Eductional (1979)

Language Teaching and Learning, 4 Science,
Colin Carré, Ward Lock Educational (1981)

Using the School's Surroundings, Stephen
Scoffham, Ward Lock Educational (1981)

The Body in Question, Jonathan Miller, Jonathan
Cape (1978)

Publications of the Association for Science
Education, College Lane, Hatfield, Herts, AL10
9AA:
APU Science Reports for Teachers
   Science at Age 11
   Assessing Practical Work

Experiencing Energy:
   Book 1 Moving Things
   Book 2 Burning, Warmth and Sunlight
   Book 3 Working with Electricity

ASE Primary Science (Issues 1-9 of the ASE
Primary Science Newsheet in a bound form)

Science and Primary Education Papers (1981)
No. 2 The Headteacher and Primary Science
No. 3 A Post of Responsibility in Science

Publications of the School Natural Science
Society available from the ASE at the above
address:
   No. 1 Nature Activities in Schools
   No. 11 The Keeping of Animals and Plants in
   Schools
   No. 16 Earthworms
   No. 26 Housing Living Things in the
   Classroom
   No. 31 Water for the Under Eights
   No. 45 Snails and Slugs
   No. 52 Primary School Sound